Plentiful
Possibilities

A Timeless Treasury of 16 Terrific Quilts

Lynda Milligan & Nancy Smith

Text and artwork ©2003 Lynda Milligan and Nancy Smith
Artwork ©2003 C&T Publishing
Editor-in-Chief: Darra Williamson
Editor: Lynn Koolish
Technical Editors: Karyn Hoyt-Culp, Linda Dease Smith
Copyeditor/Proofreader: Eva Simoni Erb, Kelly McCaw
Cover Designer: Christina Jarumay
Design Director: Diane Pedersen
Book Designer: Staci Harpole, Cubic Design
Original Illustrations: Possibilities staff
Additional Illustrations: Kirstie L. McCormick
Production Assistant: Luke Mulks
Photography: Brian Birlauf unless otherwise noted
Published by C&T Publishing, Inc., P.O. Box 1456, Lafayette, California, 94549
Front cover and title page: Photos by Garry Gay, styling by Garry Gay and Diane Pedersen
Back cover: *Cinnamon Hearts*

Library of Congress Cataloging-in-Publication Data

Milligan, Lynda
  Plentiful possibilities : a timeless treasury of 16 terrific quilts /
Lynda Milligan and Nancy Smith.
    p. cm.
  ISBN 1-57120-214-5 (Paper Trade)
  1. Patchwork--Patterns. 2. Appliqué--Patterns. 3. Quilting. I.
Smith, Nancy II. Title.
  TT835.M5328 2003
  746.46'041--dc21

                        2003006390

Printed in China
10 9 8 7 6 5 4 3 2 1

C·O·N·T·E·N·T·S

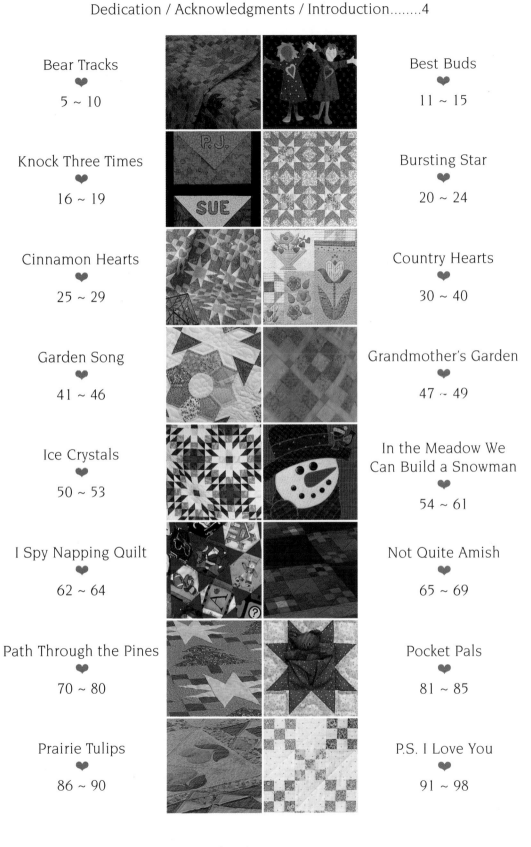

DEDICATION

To Gene Milligan and Jack Smith, our retired husbands, who had to quit their jobs in order to pursue their hobbies. We, however, have created our jobs so that we can play at our favorite hobby every day. We love you both.

Lynda & Nancy

ACKNOWLEDGMENTS

A special thanks to all of our customers and students at Great American Quilt Factory who have inspired the creativity to develop patterns and books that help others carry on the fine art of quilting.

Also, thank you to our great employees who make it enjoyable to come to work every day, and surround us with even more creativity and inspiration.

INTRODUCTION

Having written over fifty books and having made at least fifteen quilts for each book, we found choosing sixteen quilts for this book a difficult task. We made photocopies of our favorite quilts, placed them on the floor, and began the lengthy process of elimination. We wanted to choose quilts from a variety of books, representing a wide range of skill levels, as well as various techniques. We gave the list to the creative staff of C&T Publishing, who finally narrowed down the choices to these sixteen wonderful quilts. What to do with the rest of the quilts? For those remaining, there are always more Possibilities.

Finished block size: 10 $^1/_2$" x 10 $^1/_2$" (set on point)
Finished quilt size: 53" x 70"

MATERIALS AND YARDAGE

Tan 5 yards for background
Bear's Paws $^1/_4$ yard each of 12 fabrics
Rust 1 $^1/_8$ yards for chain squares
Backing 4 yards
Binding $^5/_8$ yard
Batting 59" x 76"

CUTTING

This quilt can be made using the Easy Triangles technique for the half-square triangle units. For the Easy Triangle method, you will need 24 copies of page 99. Alternate cutting directions are given if you prefer not to use Easy Triangles.

Tan fabric

Bear's Paw block backgrounds: Cut 48 rectangles 2" x 5" and 48 squares 2" x 2". Cut either 24 squares 5 $^1/_2$" x 5 $^1/_2$" for Easy Triangles *or* cut 96 squares 2 $^3/_8$" x 2 $^3/_8$", then cut each in half diagonally.
Chain block backgrounds: Cut 6 strips 2" x width of the fabric, 4 strips 3 $^1/_2$" x width of the fabric, 4 strips 5" x width of the fabric, and 2 strips 8" x width of the fabric.
Sashing backgrounds: Cut 76 rectangles 2" x 11".

Bear's Paw fabric

For each Bear's Paw: Cut 4 squares 3 $^1/_2$" x 3 $^1/_2$" and 1 square 2" x 2". Cut either 2 squares 5 $^1/_2$" x 5 $^1/_2$" for Easy Triangles *or* cut 8 squares 2 $^3/_8$" x 2 $^3/_8$", then cut each in half diagonally.

Rust fabric

Chain blocks: Cut 13 strips 2" x width of the fabric.
Sashing: Cut 31 squares 2" x 2".

Binding fabric

Cut 7 strips 2 $^1/_2$" x width of the fabric.

DIRECTIONS

Refer to Quilting Basics (pages 102–110) as needed for quilt construction techniques. Use a $^1/_4$" seam allowance unless otherwise noted.

Block Assembly

Bear's Paw Blocks

1. Make 16 half-square triangle units for each block using the background and Bear's Paw block fabrics. Use the 1 $^1/_2$" Finished Easy Triangles (refer to page 99) or piece together triangles cut from the 2 $^3/_8$" squares.

Make 16 per block.

2. Make 12 blocks as shown. For each block:

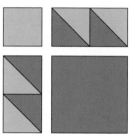

Make 4 per block.

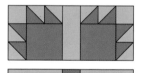

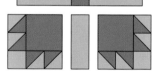

Stitch block together.

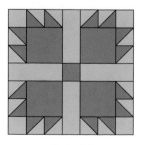

Make 12.

Press after each step.

Chain Blocks

1. Make 2 strip sets each A, B, and C, and 1 strip set D. Press.

2. Crosscut strip sets into 2" segments.

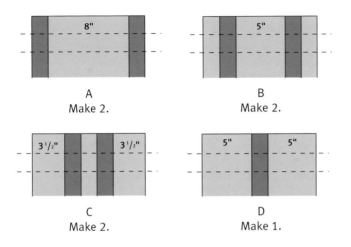

A
Make 2.

B
Make 2.

C
Make 2.

D
Make 1.

3. Make 20 blocks as shown. Press seams in one direction.

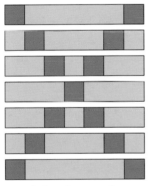

Stitch strips together.

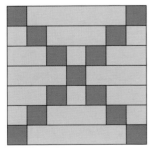

Make 20.

Quilt Assembly

Refer to the Quilt Assembly Diagram.

1. Stitch the Bear's Paw blocks, chain blocks, and sashing strips into diagonal rows. Press.

2. Stitch the sashing rectangles and chain squares into rows. Press.

3. Stitch the rows together. Press.

4. Trim the edges of the quilt ³/₈" outside the corners of the chain squares, as shown.

Finishing

1. Piece the backing so it is the same size as the batting. Layer and quilt as desired. Trim the backing and batting even with the quilt top.

2. Bind the quilt using a ³/₈" seam allowance. Refer to pages 109–110 for information on bindings.

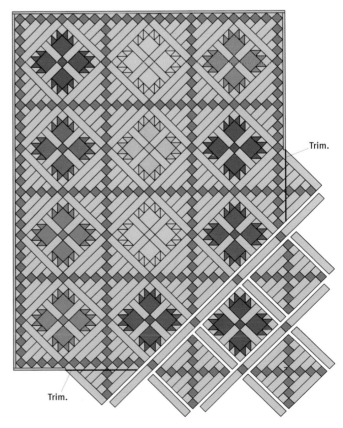

Quilt Assembly Diagram

TIE PILLOW

Finished pillow size: 13" x 13"

MATERIALS AND YARDAGE

Striped 1/2 yard
Rust 1/2 yard
Pillow form 14" x 14"

CUTTING

Striped fabric
Cut 1 square 13 1/2" x 13 1/2".
Cut 2 pillow tie pieces using the pattern on page 10.

Rust fabric
Cut 1 square 13 1/2" x 13 1/2".
Cut 2 pillow tie pieces using the pattern on page 10.

DIRECTIONS

Use a 1/4" seam allowance unless otherwise noted.

1. Place 1 striped and 1 rust tie piece, right sides together. Stitch a 1/4" seam around the curved edge. Turn right side out and press. Repeat with the other 2 tie pieces.

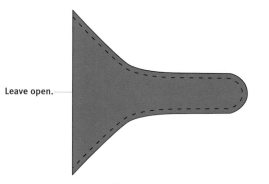

Leave open.

Stitch curved edges.

2. Place the striped square right side up. Place 1 tie on the square, raw edges even, with the striped side down. Pin through all 3 layers. Fold up the tie end, and pin it to the center of the square. Repeat with the other tie on the opposite side of the square. Stitch each tie to the square through all layers using a scant 1/4" seam.

3. With the tie ends still pinned to the center, place the striped square on the rust square, right sides together. Pin all raw edges.

4. Stitch around 3 sides of the square, leaving one of the sides with a tie open for turning. Trim the corners, and turn right side out. Unpin the tie ends and press.

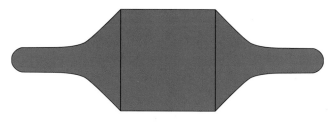

Turn right side out.

5. Insert the pillow form. Hand stitch the opening closed.

6. Tie the ends together.

BEAR TRACKS PILLOW

Finished pillow size: 13 $1/2$" x 13 $1/2$"

MATERIALS AND YARDAGE

Tan $1/3$ yard for background
Bear's Paw $1/4$ yard
Rust $1/8$ yard for corner setting squares
Pillow back $1/2$ yard
Pillow form 14" x 14"

CUTTING

This pillow can be made using the Easy Triangles technique for the half-square triangle units. For the Easy Triangle method, you will need 2 copies of page 99. Alternate cutting directions are given if you prefer not to use Easy Triangles.

Tan fabric

Background fabric: Cut 4 rectangles 2" x 5", 4 squares 2" x 2", and 4 rectangles 2" x 11". Cut either 2 squares 5 $1/2$" x 5 $1/2$" for Easy Triangles **or** cut 8 squares 2 $3/8$" x 2 $3/8$", then cut each in half diagonally.

Bear's Paw fabric

Bear's Paw: Cut 4 squares 3 $1/2$" x 3 $1/2$" and 1 square 2" x 2". Cut either 2 squares 5 $1/2$" x 5 $1/2$" for Easy Triangles **or** cut 8 squares 2 $3/8$" x 2 $3/8$", then cut each in half diagonally.

Rust fabric

Corner setting squares: Cut 4 squares 2" x 2".

Pillow back fabric

Cut 2 rectangles 14" x 20".

DIRECTIONS

Use a $1/4$" seam allowance unless otherwise noted.

1. Refer to Bear's Paw Blocks on page 6 to make one Bear's Paw block. Make 16 half-square triangle units for the block.

2. Stitch a 2" x 11" rectangle to each side of the Bear's Paw block. Stitch corner setting squares to each end of the remaining 2" x 11" rectangles. Stitch them to the top and bottom of the block. Press.

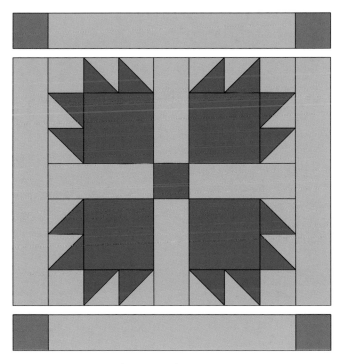

Pillow Assembly Diagram

3. Make the envelope back by pressing each pillow back piece in half, wrong sides together. When folded, each will measure 14" x 10". Place both pieces on the right side of the pillow top, matching raw edges and overlapping the folded edges in the center. Pin in place. Stitch around all 4 sides. Clip the corners, turn right side out, and press.

4. Insert the pillow form.

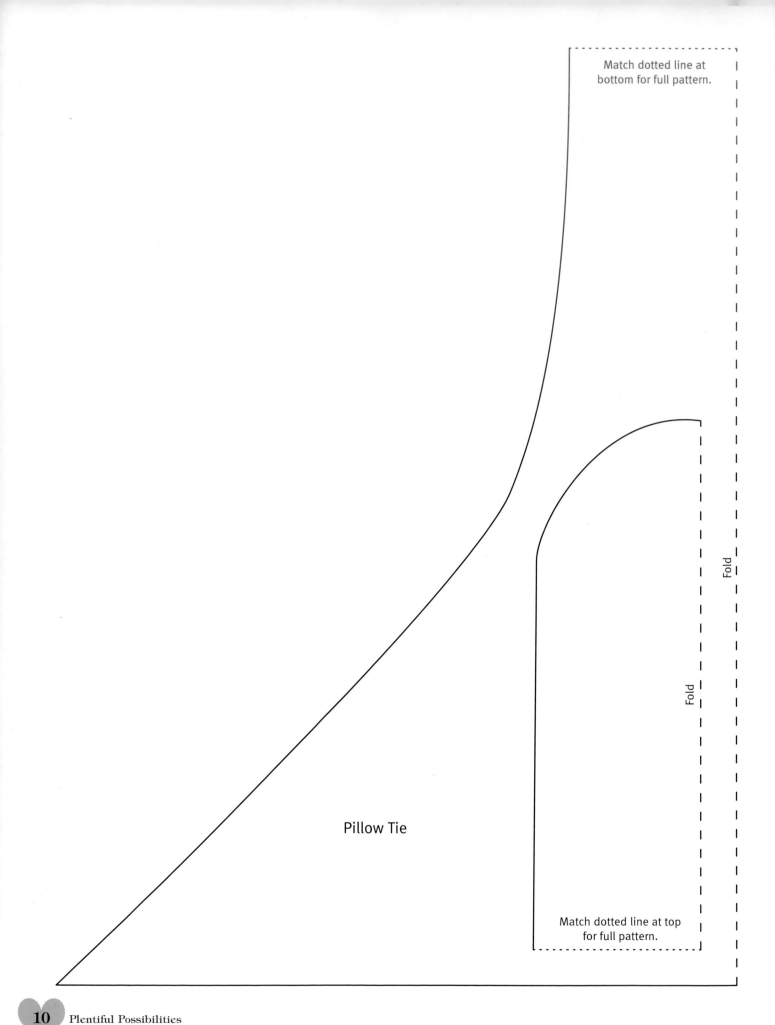

Match dotted line at
bottom for full pattern.

Fold

Fold

Pillow Tie

Match dotted line at top
for full pattern.

Finished block size: 12" x 12"
Finished quilt size: 59" x 59"

MATERIALS AND YARDAGE

Black print 1 ³/₈ yards for block backgrounds

Appliqués ¹/₆ yard each (or scraps at least 6" x 8") of 9 or more fabrics for dresses, and ¹/₈ yard each (or small scraps) for faces, hands, hair, hearts, and stockings

Fuchsia ³/₄ yard for sashing and corner squares

Teal ¹/₂ yard for Border 1

Purple ³/₄ yard for Border 2

Black solid 1 ⁵/₈ yards for Borders 2 and 3

Backing 3 ⁷/₈ yards

Binding ⁵/₈ yard

Batting 65" x 65"

Fusible web (optional for fusible appliqué)

Permanent markers for eyes and nose

Blush makeup for cheeks

CUTTING

This quilt can be made using the Easy Triangles technique for the half-square triangle units. For the Easy Triangle method, you will need 30 copies of page 99. Alternate cutting directions are given if you prefer not to use Easy Triangles.

NOTE: *The pieced border in this quilt requires exact piecing of all the elements, so exact lengths for all pieces of the quilt, except Border 3, are given in the cutting instructions.*

Black print fabric
Block backgrounds: Cut 9 squares 12 ¹/₂" x 12 ¹/₂".

Appliqué fabrics
Cut 9 sets using the patterns on pages 14–15.

Fuchsia fabric
Sashing: Cut 9 strips 2" x width of the fabric; seam together end-to-end, then cut into:
  6 pieces 12 ¹/₂" long for the vertical sashing
  4 pieces 39 ¹/₂" long for the horizontal and side sashing
  2 pieces 42 ¹/₂" long for the top and bottom sashing.
Border 2: Cut 4 squares 3 ¹/₂" x 3 ¹/₂".

Teal fabric
Border 1: Cut 5 strips 2" x width of the fabric; seam together end-to-end as needed, then cut into:
  2 pieces 42 ¹/₂" long for the side borders
  2 pieces 45 ¹/₂" long for the top and bottom borders.

Purple fabric
Border 2: Cut 30 squares 5 ¹/₂" x 5 ¹/₂" for Easy Triangles *or* 120 squares 2 ³/₈" x 2 ³/₈", then cut each in half diagonally.

Black solid fabric
Border 2: Cut 30 squares 5 ¹/₂" x 5 ¹/₂" for Easy Triangles *or* 120 squares 2 ³/₈" x 2 ³/₈", then cut each in half diagonally.
Border 3: Cut 6 strips 4 ¹/₂" x width of the fabric.

Binding fabric
Cut 7 strips 2 ¹/₂" x width of the fabric.

DIRECTIONS

Refer to Quilting Basics (pages 102–110) as needed for quilt construction techniques. Use a ¹/₄" seam allowance unless otherwise noted.

Block Assembly

1. Appliqué the blocks as shown. Leave the hands unstitched or unfused until after the blocks are stitched to the sashing.

Leave hands free until sashing is complete. Make 9.

2. Use permanent marker for the eyes and nose, and blush makeup for the cheeks.

Quilt Assembly

Refer to the Quilt Assembly Diagram.

1. Stitch the blocks and vertical sashing pieces into rows, keeping the hands out of the seam allowances.

2. Stitch the rows together with the horizontal sashing between them.

3. Stitch the side sashing to the quilt top. Press.

4. Stitch the top and bottom sashing to the quilt top. Press.

5. Finish appliquéing the hands.

Border 1

1. Stitch the Border 1 side strips to the quilt top. Press. Stitch the Border 1 top and bottom strips to the quilt top. Press.

Border 2

1. Make 240 half-square triangle units by using the 1¹/₂" Finished Easy Triangles (refer to page 99), or by stitching together the black and purple triangles. Press.

Make 240.

2. Stitch the half-square triangle units together in pairs to make Flying Geese. Press.

Make 120.

3. Stitch the Flying Geese together into 4 borders of 30 units each. Press.

4. Stitch the side borders to the quilt, purple triangles pointing as shown in the Quilt Assembly Diagram. Press.

5. Stitch the 3¹/₂" fuchsia squares to the ends of the remaining 2 borders. Stitch the top and bottom borders to the quilt, purple triangles pointing as shown. Press.

Border 3

1. Measure the length of the quilt. Piece and cut the Border 3 strips to the measured length and stitch to the sides of the quilt. Press. Measure the width of the quilt (including the side borders). Piece and cut the Border 3 strips to the measured length, and stitch to the top and bottom of the quilt. Press.

Finishing

1. Piece the backing so it is the same size as the batting. Layer and quilt as desired. Trim the backing and batting even with the quilt top.

2. Bind the quilt using a ³/₈" seam allowance. Refer to pages 109–110 for information on bindings.

Quilt Assembly Diagram

Patterns are reversed for tracing to fusible web.

Use blush makeup for cheeks.
Use permanent marker for nose and eyes.

Cut 9.

Cut 9 reversed.

Patterns are reversed for tracing to fusible web.

Cut 3, reversing as desired.

Cut 3, reversing as desired.

Cut 3, reversing as desired.

Cut 3, reversing as desired.

Cut 3, reversing as desired.

Cut 3, reversing as desired.

Finished quilt size: 23" x 23"

MATERIALS AND YARDAGE

Black ½ yard for background

Brights ¼ yard each of 8 fabrics for envelopes, envelope flaps, lettering, notepad, and pencil pocket

Red ¼ yard for notepad pocket

Yellow ⅛ yard for border

Blue ⅛ yard for border

Backing ⅞ yard

Binding ⅓ yard

Batting 27" x 27"

Fusible web optional for fusible appliqué

CUTTING

Black fabric

Background: Cut 1 rectangle 23½" x 8½" for the top, 1 rectangle 7½" x 12½" for the left side, 6 rectangles 1½" x 5" for the sashing, and 3 rectangles 1½" x 16½" for the sashing.

Bright fabrics

Name envelopes: Cut 4 rectangles 5" x 7" for the backs, 8 squares 5½" x 5½" for the sides, and 4 rectangles 3¾" x 7" for the flaps.

Letters: Use the patterns on pages 18–19.

Notepad and pencil pocket: Cut 1 rectangle 5½" x 3" for the flap, and 1 rectangle 3½" x 4½" for the pencil pocket.

Red fabric

Notepad pocket: Cut 1 rectangle 5½" x 15".

Yellow fabric

Borders: Cut 35 squares 1½" x 1½".

Blue fabric

Borders: Cut 35 squares 1½" x 1½".

Binding fabric

Cut 3 strips 2½" x width of the fabric.

DIRECTIONS

Refer to Quilting Basics (pages 102–110) as needed for quilt construction techniques. Use a ¼" seam allowance unless otherwise noted.

Envelope Blocks

1. Press 2 side pieces in half diagonally, wrong sides together. Pin the side pieces to the right side of the back piece with the bottom corners matching and the points extending at the top. Pin the side pieces together at the overlap, but do not pin through the back piece.

Pin at overlap.

2. Remove the side pieces from the back and stitch close to the edge along the diagonal overlap.

Stitch along overlap.

3. Place the sides on the back piece again. Stitch the side and bottom edges together ⅛" from the edge.

Stitch sides.

4. Fold the flap piece in half, right sides together, to form a 3 ½" x 3 ¾" rectangle. Stitch one 3 ½" edge. Trim the point.

Trim.

Stitch 1 edge.

5. Turn right side out and position the seam in the center. Press.

Turn and press.

6. Appliqué the name on the flap. Pin the flap to the top edge of the envelope block, raw edges even, and stitch ⅛" from the edge. Trim the points.

Trim. — Trim.

Appliqué, stitch, and trim.

7. Make 3 more envelope blocks.

Notepad and Pencil Pocket

1. Fold the pencil pocket piece in half, right sides together, to form a 1 ¾" x 4 ½" rectangle. Stitch the 3 open sides, leaving an opening on the long side for turning. Clip, turn, and press.

2. As in Envelope Blocks, Steps 4 and 5, fold the notepad flap piece in half, right sides together, to form a 2 ¾" x 3" rectangle. Stitch one 2 ¾" side. Trim the point. Turn right side out, place the seam in the center, and press.

3. Place the notepad flap, right sides together, at one end of the notepad pocket piece.

4. Fold the notepad pocket piece in half, right sides together, to form a 5 ½" x 7 ½" rectangle. Stitch the 3 open sides, catching the flap in the seam and leaving an opening on the side for turning. Trim the corners, turn, and press.

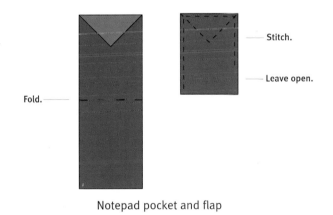

Fold.

Stitch.

Leave open.

Notepad pocket and flap

Quilt Assembly

Refer to the Quilt Assembly Diagram.

1. Stitch the envelope blocks and sashing strips into rows. Press.

2. Stitch the rows together with sashing strips between the rows. Press.

3. Stitch the pencil pocket to the notepad pocket. Stitch the notepad pocket to the notepad pocket background.

4. Stitch the notepad pocket background piece to the left of the envelope blocks section.

5. Stitch the yellow and blue 1 ½" squares into 3 rows of 23 squares each. Press. Stitch one row of squares to the top of the envelope row. Stitch one row of squares to the bottom of the envelope row. Press.

6. Stitch the 8 ½" x 23 ½" background piece to the top of the quilt. Press.

7. Stitch the remaining row of yellow and blue squares to the top of the quilt. Press.

8. Appliqué the lettering to the background.

Finishing

1. Cut the backing so it is the same size as the batting. Layer and quilt as desired. Trim the backing and batting even with the quilt top.

2. Bind the quilt using a ⅜" seam allowance. Refer to pages 109–110 for information on bindings.

Quilt Assembly Diagram

Patterns are reversed for tracing to fusible web.

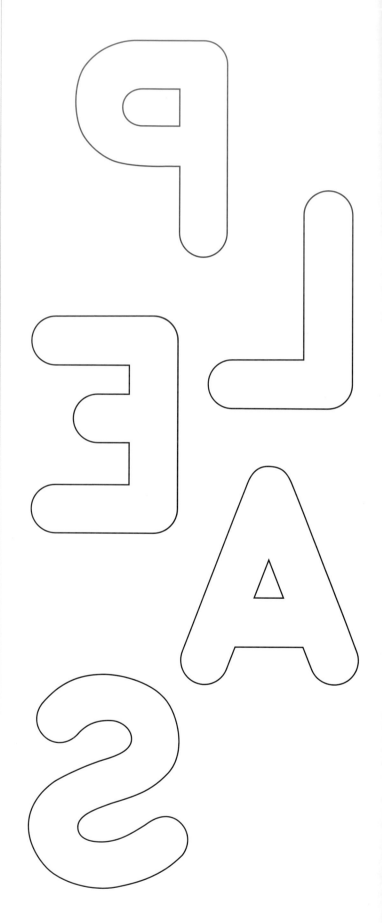

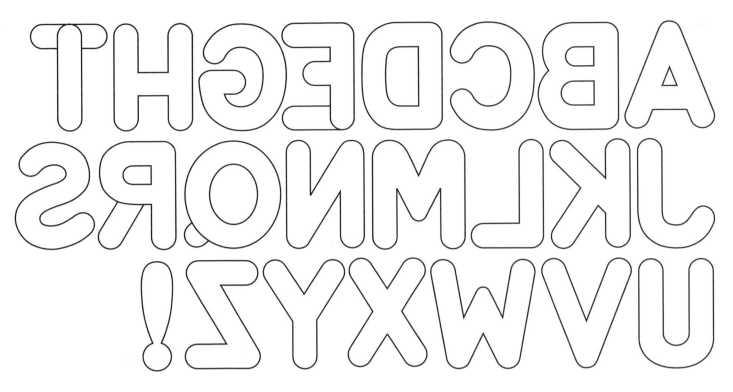

QUILT LABEL

1. Cut a piece of fabric 2" larger than the label and iron freezer paper to the wrong side of the fabric.

2. Make a copy of the label.

3. Using the copy of the label, trace the design onto the fabric with a permanent pen. Use a window or light box to make it easier to see the design.

4. Use colored permanent pens to color as desired.

5. Remove the freezer paper. Cut out the label ½" from the outer line and turn the edges under ¼".

6. Stitch the label to the back of the quilt.

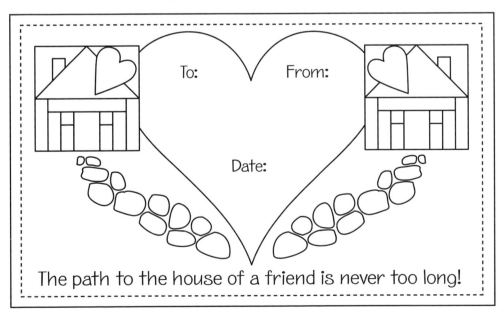

To: From:

Date:

The path to the house of a friend is never too long!

B·U·R·S·T·I·N·G S·T·A·R

Finished block size: 18" x 18"
Finished quilt size: 72" x 90"

MATERIALS AND YARDAGE

Floral print $^1/_2$ yard for star centers, $2^1/_4$ yards for
  Border 2
Pink 1 yard for inner star points
Green print $2^7/_8$ yards for outer stars
Beige $2^1/_4$ yards for background
Green $^5/_8$ yard for Border 1
Backing $5^5/_8$ yards
Binding $^3/_4$ yard
Batting 78" x 96"

CUTTING

This quilt can be made using the Easy Triangles
technique for the half-square triangle star points. For
the Easy Triangle method, you will need 36 copies of
page 101. Alternate cutting directions are given if you
prefer not to use Easy Triangles.

Floral print fabric
Star centers: Cut 12 squares $6^1/_2$" x $6^1/_2$".
Border 2: Cut 8 strips 8" x width of the fabric.

Pink fabric
Inner star points: Cut 12 squares $8^1/_2$" x $8^1/_2$" for
  Easy Triangles **or** Cut 48 squares $3^7/_8$" x $3^7/_8$", then
  cut each in half diagonally.

Green print fabric
Outer stars: Cut 36 squares $8^1/_2$" x $8^1/_2$" for Easy
  Triangles **or** cut 144 squares $3^7/_8$" x $3^7/_8$", then cut
  each in half diagonally.

Beige fabric
Background: Cut 48 squares $3^1/_2$" x $3^1/_2$". Cut 24
  squares $8^1/_2$" x $8^1/_2$" for Easy Triangles **or** cut 96
  squares $3^7/_8$" x $3^7/_8$", then cut each in half diagonally.

Green fabric
Border 1: Cut 8 strips 2" x width of the fabric.

Binding fabric
Cut 9 strips $2^1/_2$" x width of the fabric.

DIRECTIONS

*Refer to Quilting Basics (pages 102–110) as needed for
quilt construction techniques. Use a $^1/_4$" seam allowance unless
otherwise noted.*

Block Assembly

1. Make 96 half-square triangle units using the inner
star point and outer star fabrics. Use the 3" Finished
Easy Triangles (refer to page 101), or piece together
triangles cut from the $3^7/_8$" squares.

Make 96.

2. Make 192 half-square triangle units using the outer
star and background fabrics. Use the 3" Finished
Easy Triangles (refer to page 101) or piece together
triangles cut from the $3^7/_8$" squares.

Make 192.

3. Make 12 blocks as shown. Press.

Make 48.

Make 48.

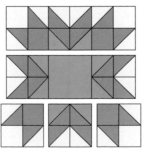

Stitch block together.

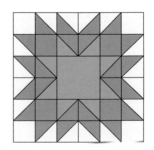

Make 12.

Quilt Assembly

Refer to the Quilt Assembly Diagram.

1. Stitch the blocks together into rows. Press the seam allowances in alternate directions for each row, so the seams nest when the rows are stitched together.

2. Stitch the rows together. Press.

Borders

1. Measure the length of the quilt. Piece and cut the Border 1 strips to the measured length, and stitch to the sides of the quilt. Press. Measure the width of the quilt (including the side borders). Piece and cut the Border 1 strips to the measured length, and stitch to the top and bottom of the quilt. Press.

2. Measure the length of the quilt. Piece and cut the Border 2 strips to the measured length, and stitch to the sides of the quilt. Press. Measure the width of the quilt (including the side borders). Piece and cut the Border 2 strips to the measured length, and stitch to the top and bottom of the quilt. Press.

Finishing

1. Piece the backing so it is the same size as the batting. Layer and quilt as desired. Trim the backing and batting even with the quilt top.

2. Bind the quilt using a ³/₈" seam allowance. Refer to pages 109–110 for information on bindings.

Quilt Assembly Diagram

BURSTING STAR THROW PILLOW

Finished Size: 18" x 18"

MATERIALS AND YARDAGE

Floral print ¹/₄ yard for star center
Pink ¹/₃ yard for inner star points
Green print ¹/₃ yard for outer star
Beige ¹/₃ yard for background
Backing for quilting ²/₃ yard
Pillow back ⁷/₈ yard
Binding ¹/₄ yard
Batting 22" x 22"
Pillow form 18" x 18"

CUTTING

This pillow can be made using the Easy Triangles technique for the half-square triangle star points. For the Easy Triangle method, you will need 3 copies of page 101. Alternate cutting directions are given if you prefer not to use Easy Triangles.

Floral print fabric
Star center: Cut 1 square 6¹/₂" x 6¹/₂".

Pink fabric

Inner star points: Cut 1 square 8 ½" x 8 ½" for Easy Triangles **or** cut 4 squares 3 ⅞" x 3 ⅞", then cut each in half diagonally.

Green print fabric

Outer star: Cut 4 squares 3 ½" x 3 ½". Cut 3 squares 8 ½" x 8 ½" for Easy Triangles **or** cut 12 squares 3 ⅞" x 3 ⅞", then cut each in half diagonally.

Beige fabric

Background: Cut 4 squares 3 ½" x 3 ½". Cut 2 squares 8 ½" x 8 ½" for Easy Triangles **or** cut 8 squares 3 ⅞" x 3 ⅞", then cut each in half diagonally.

Backing for quilting

Cut 1 square 22" x 22".

Pillow back fabric

Cut 2 rectangles 18 ½" x 27".

Binding fabric

Cut 2 strips 2 ¼" x width of the fabric.

DIRECTIONS

Use a ¼" seam allowance unless otherwise noted.

1. Make 8 half-square triangle units using the inner star point fabric and the outer star fabric. Make 16 half-square triangle units using the outer star fabric and the background fabric. Use 3" Finished Easy Triangles (refer to page 101), or piece together triangles cut from the 3 ⅞" squares.

2. Piece the block as described in Block Assembly on page 21.

3. Layer the block with the batting and the backing fabric. Quilt as desired.

4. Trim the backing and batting to the same size as the pillow top.

5. Make the envelope back by pressing each pillow back piece in half, wrong sides together. When folded, each will measure 13 ½" x 18 ½". Place both pieces on the wrong side of the pillow top, matching raw edges and overlapping the folded edges in the center. Baste around all 4 sides.

6. Bind the pillow using a ¼" seam allowance. Refer to pages 109–110 for information on bindings.

7. Insert the pillow form.

BURSTING STAR PILLOWCASE

Finished size: 20" x 29"

MATERIALS AND YARDAGE

For one pillowcase:

Pink floral ⅞ yard for pillowcase
Beige ⅓ yard for light Sawtooth fabric
Green print ⅓ yard for dark Sawtooth fabric
Backing 1 ⅜ yards
Binding ⅛ yard
Batting 34" x 45"

CUTTING

This pillow can be made using the Easy Triangles technique for the half-square triangle star points. For the Easy Triangle method, you will need 2 copies of page 101. Alternate cutting directions are given if you prefer not to use Easy Triangles.

Pink floral fabric

Pillowcase: Cut 1 rectangle 20 ½" x 41" and 1 rectangle 4 ½" x 41".

Cutting (continued)

Beige fabric

Vertical band: Cut 1 rectangle 1 1/2" x 41".
Sawtooth insert: Cut 2 squares 8 1/2" x 8 1/2" for Easy
  Triangles **or** cut 7 squares 3 7/8" x 3 7/8", then cut each
  in half diagonally.

Green print fabric

Vertical band: Cut 1 rectangle 1 1/2" x 41".
Sawtooth insert: Cut 2 squares 8 1/2" x 8 1/2" for Easy
  Triangles **or** cut 7 squares 3 7/8" x 3 7/8", then cut each
  in half diagonally.

Backing fabric

Cut 1 rectangle 34" x 45".

Binding fabric

Cut 1 strip 2 1/2" x width of the fabric.

DIRECTIONS

Use a 1/4" seam allowance unless otherwise noted.

Sawtooth Inserts

1. Make 14 half-square triangle units with the
Sawtooth fabrics. Use the 3" Finished Easy Triangles
(refer to page 101), or piece together triangles cut
from the 3 7/8" squares.

Make 14.

2. Stitch the half-square triangle units into a row. Press.

3. Center the dark side of the Sawtooth insert on the
beige 1 1/2" x 41" rectangle. Stitch. Trim the ends of
the Sawtooth insert. Stitch the green print 1 1/2" x 41"
rectangle to the other side of the Sawtooth insert.
Press.

Pillowcase Assembly

1. Stitch the pillowcase fabric rectangle and the 4 1/2"
rectangle to the Sawtooth insert. Press.

2. Layer with batting and backing. Quilt as
desired. Trim the backing and batting even with the
pillow top.

3. Fold the pillowcase in half, right sides together.
Use a **1/2"** seam allowance to stitch the long side and
the short side farthest from the Sawtooth insert. Turn
the pillowcase right side out. Press.

4. Bind the raw edge of the pillowcase using a 3/8" seam
allowance. Refer to pages 109–110 for information
on bindings.

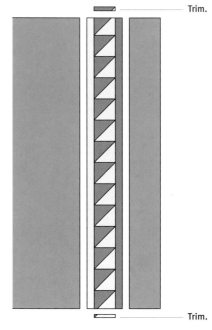

Pillowcase Assembly Diagram

Finished block size: 9" x 9"
Finished quilt size: 59" x 77"

Use traditional templates to make this block or try your hand at paper piecing. Refer to pages 104–105 for information on paper piecing.

MATERIALS AND YARDAGE

Dark peach 3 yards for star backgrounds and half-square triangles

Cream 2 1/2 yards for star points, star centers, and Border 1

Light peach 2 1/4 yards for star points and star centers

Lavender 7/8 yard for Four-Patch blocks

Light green 1 1/2 yards for Four-Patch blocks and Border 2

Medium green 7/8 yard for half-square triangles

Light peachy pink 1/6 yard for heart appliqués

Medium peachy pink 1/6 yard for heart appliqués

Backing 4 yards

Binding 3/4 yard

Batting 65" x 83"

Fusible web (optional for fusible appliqué)

CUTTING

Patterns are on page 29.

This quilt can be made using the Easy Triangles technique for the half-square triangle units. For the Easy Triangle method, you will need 12 copies of page 101. Alternate cutting directions are given if you prefer not to use Easy Triangles.

Dark peach fabric

Star backgrounds: Cut 164 Pattern A *or* use the paper-piecing pattern.

Half-square triangles: Cut 12 squares 8 1/2" x 8 1/2" for Easy Triangles *or* cut 48 squares 3 7/8" x 3 7/8", then cut each in half diagonally.

Cream fabric

Star centers: Cut 17 squares 3 1/2" x 3 1/2".

Block A star points: Cut 82 using pattern B and 82 using pattern B reversed *or* use the paper-piecing pattern.

Border 1: Cut 7 strips 1 1/2" x width of the fabric.

Light peach fabric

Star centers: Cut 18 squares 3 1/2" x 3 1/2".

Block B star points: Cut 82 using pattern B and 82 using pattern B reversed *or* use the paper-piecing pattern.

Lavender fabric

Four-Patch blocks: Cut 10 strips 2" x width of the fabric.

Light green fabric

Four-Patch blocks: Cut 10 strips 2" x width of the fabric.

Border 2: Cut 7 strips 3 1/2" x width of the fabric.

Medium green fabric

Half-square triangles: Cut 12 squares 8 1/2" x 8 1/2" for Easy Triangles *or* cut 48 squares 3 7/8" x 3 7/8", then cut each in half diagonally.

Light peachy pink fabric

Appliqué hearts: Cut 18 using the heart pattern.

Medium peachy pink fabric

Appliqué hearts: Cut 17 using the heart pattern.

Binding fabric

Cut 7 to 8 strips 2 1/2" x width of the fabric.

DIRECTIONS

Refer to Quilting Basics (pages 102–110) as needed for quilt construction techniques. Use a 1/4" seam allowance unless otherwise noted.

Block Assembly

Block A

1. Make 72 half-square triangle units using the dark peach and medium green fabrics. Use the 3" Finished Easy Triangles (refer to page 101), or piece together triangles cut from the 3 7/8" squares.

Make 72.

2. Make 72 star point units using the dark peach and cream fabrics. Use patterns A and B or the optional paper-piecing pattern on page 29. Press seams toward the darker fabric.

Make 72.

3. Make 18 blocks as shown. Press.

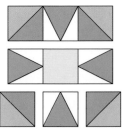 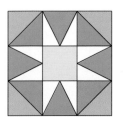

Stitch block together.   Make 18.

Block B

1. Make 10 strip sets using the lavender and the light green 2" strips.

Make 10.

2. Crosscut the strip sets into 2" segments. Make 68 Four-Patch blocks from the segments.

Make 68.

3. Make 68 star point units using the dark peach and light peach fabrics. Use patterns A and B or the optional paper-piecing pattern on page 29. Press seams toward the darker fabric.

Make 68.

4. Make 17 blocks as shown. Press.

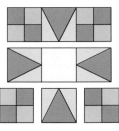 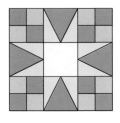

Stitch block together.   Make 17.

Appliqué

1. Appliqué the hearts to the blocks. Use the light peachy pink hearts for Block A and the medium peachy pink hearts for Block B.

Finishing Row

1. Make 24 half-square triangle units using the dark peach and medium green fabrics. Use the 3" Finished Easy Triangles (refer to page 101), or piece together triangles cut from the 3 7/8" squares.

Make 24.

2. Make 28 Four-Patch blocks using the lavender and the light green 2" strips.

Make 28.

3. Make 14 star point units using the dark peach and light peach fabrics. Use patterns A and B or the optional paper-piecing pattern on page 29. Press seams toward the darker fabric.

Make 14.

4. Make 10 star point units using the dark peach and cream fabrics. Use patterns A and B or the optional paper-piecing pattern on page 29. Press seams toward the darker fabric.

Make 10.

5. Make 10 Partial Block A as shown. Press toward the darker fabric.

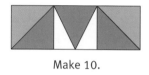

Make 10.

6. Make 14 Partial Block B as shown. Press toward the darker fabric.

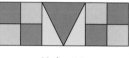

Make 14.

Quilt Assembly

Refer to the Quilt Assembly Diagram.

1. Arrange the blocks, alternating A and B blocks. Carefully place the partial blocks around the edge to finish the large "shield shapes" around the stars.

2. Place the 4 remaining half-square triangle units from Finishing Row Step 1 at the corners of the quilt top.

3. Stitch the blocks into horizontal rows, as shown. Press the seam allowances in alternate directions for each row, so the seams nest when the rows are stitched together.

4. Stitch the rows together. Press the seams in one direction.

Borders

1. Measure the length of the quilt. Piece and cut the Border 1 strips to the measured length, and stitch to the sides of the quilt. Measure the width of the quilt (including the side borders). Piece and cut the Border 1 strips to the measured length, and stitch to the top and bottom of the quilt. Press.

2. Measure the length of the quilt. Piece and cut the Border 2 strips to the measured length, and stitch to the sides of the quilt. Measure the width of the quilt (including the side borders). Piece and cut the Border 2 strips to the measured length, and stitch to the top and bottom of the quilt. Press.

Finishing

1. Piece the backing so it is the same size as the batting. Layer and quilt as desired. Trim the backing and batting even with the quilt top.

2. Bind the quilt using a $^3/_8$" seam allowance. Refer to pages 109–110 for information on bindings.

Quilt Assembly Diagram

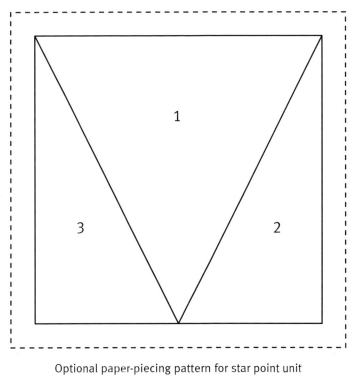

Optional paper-piecing pattern for star point unit
Make 164 copies.

Pattern is reversed for tracing to fusible web.

Cut 18 light peachy pink and 17 medium peachy pink.

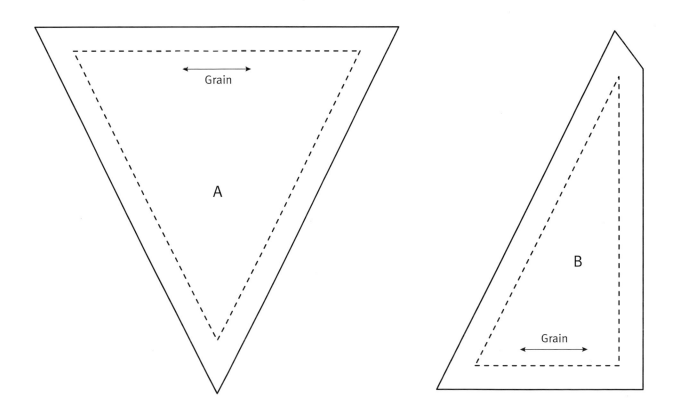

Photo by Diane Pedersen

Finished quilt size: 42" x 54"

MATERIALS AND YARDAGE

Refer to Block Names Diagram on page 32 for block numbers and letters.

Cream ⅝ yard for Border 2, Blocks 3, 7, B, and C
Yellow #1 ¼ yards for Blocks 9 and A
Yellow #2 ⅓ yard for Blocks 1, 11, and B
Yellow #3 ½ yard for Border 2 and filler strips
Pink #1 ¼ yard for filler strip
Pink #2 ¼ yard for Block C
Pink #3 ¼ yard for filler strips
Pink #4 ⅜ yard for Border 2, Block C, and filler strip
Blue #1 ⅓ yard for Blocks 6, 8, A, and B
Blue #2 ⅛ yard for Block B and filler strip
Blue #3 1¼ yards for Border 2, Blocks 4, 10, A, B, and filler strip
Green #1 ⅝ yard for Blocks 4, 5, 12, and Border 2 corners
Green #2 ½ yard for Border 2 and Block 2
Green #3 ¼ yard for filler strip
Blue ¾ yard for Borders 1 and 3
Backing 2⅞ yards
Binding ⅝ yard
Batting 48" x 60"
Fusible web (optional for fusible appliqué)

CUTTING

Cream fabric
Border 2: Cut 1 strip 2½" x width of the fabric.
Block 3: Cut 1 rectangle 6½" x 12½".
Block 7: Cut 1 rectangle 8½" x 10½".
Blocks B and C: Cut 8 squares 2½" x 2½".
Blocks B, C, and filler strip: Cut 9 squares 2⅞" x 2⅞", then cut each in half diagonally.

Yellow #1 fabric
Block 9: Cut 1 rectangle 8½" x 4½".
Block A: Cut 2 squares 2⅞", then cut each in half diagonally.

Yellow #2 fabric
Block 1: Cut 1 rectangle 12½" x 6½".
Block 11: Cut 1 rectangle 6½" x 10½".
Block B: Cut 2 squares 2⅞" x 2⅞", then cut each in half diagonally.

Yellow #3 fabric
Border 2: Cut 2 strips 2½" x width of the fabric.
Filler strips: Cut 1 rectangle 1½" x 8½" and cut 7 squares 2⅞" x 2⅞", then cut each in half diagonally.

Pink #1 fabric
Filler strip: Cut 7 squares 2⅞" x 2⅞", then cut each in half diagonally.

Pink #2 fabric
Block C: Cut 1 square 2½" x 2½".

Pink #3 fabric
Filler strips: Cut 1 rectangle 1½" x 12½" and 1 rectangle 1½" x 10½".

Pink #4 fabric
Border 2: Cut 2 strips 2½" x width of the fabric.
Filler strip and Block C: Cut 7 squares 2⅞" x 2⅞", then cut each in half diagonally.

Blue #1 fabric
Block 6: Cut 1 rectangle 10½" x 4½".
Block 8: Cut 1 rectangle 8½" x 6½".
Block A: Cut 3 squares 2⅞" x 2⅞", then cut each in half diagonally.
Block B: Cut 2 squares 2½" x 2½".

Blue #2 fabric
Block B: Cut 2 squares 2½" x 2½".
Filler strip: Cut 1 rectangle 1½" x 12½".

Cutting (continued)

Blue #3 fabric

Border 2: Cut 7 strips 2 1/2" x width of the fabric.

Block A: Cut 1 square 6 7/8" x 6 7/8", then cut it in half diagonally.

Block 4: Cut 1 square 6 1/4" x 6 1/4". Cut 2 squares 4 7/8" x 4 7/8", then cut the 4 7/8" squares in half diagonally.

Block B: Cut 4 squares 2 7/8" x 2 7/8", then cut each in half diagonally.

Filler strip: Cut 1 rectangle 1 1/2" x 10 1/2".

Block 10: Cut 1 rectangle 6 1/2" x 4 1/2".

Green #1 fabric

Block 5: Cut 1 square 10 1/2" x 10 1/2".

Block 4: Cut 1 square 6 1/4" x 6 1/4". Cut 2 squares 4 7/8" x 4 7/8", then cut the 4 7/8" squares in half diagonally.

Block 12: Cut 1 rectangle 8 1/2" x14 1/2".

Corners of Border 2: Cut 4 squares 4 1/2" x 4 1/2".

Green #2 fabric

Border 2: Cut 2 strips 2 1/2" x width of the fabric.

Block 2: Cut 1 square 8 1/2" x 8 1/2".

Green #3 fabric

Filler strip: Cut 1 rectangle 1 1/2" x 8 1/2".

Blue fabric

Border 1: Cut 4 strips 1 1/2" x width of the fabric.

Border 3: Cut 5 strips 2 1/2" x width of the fabric.

Binding fabric

Cut 5 to 6 strips 2 1/2" x width of the fabric.

Appliqué fabrics

Patterns are on pages 35–40. Use fabric left over from the blocks.

DIRECTIONS

Refer to Quilting Basics (pages 102–110) as needed for quilt construction techniques. Use a 1/4" seam allowance unless otherwise noted.

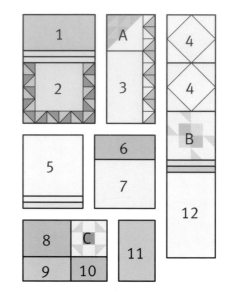

Block Names Diagram

Block Assembly

Refer to Block Names Diagram above for block numbers and letters.

1. Make 2 Block 4 as shown. Press.

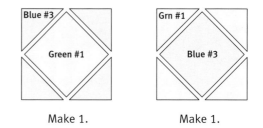

Make 1.   Make 1.

2. Make 1 Block A as shown. Press.

Make 3.

Stitch block together.

3. Make 1 Block B as shown. Press.

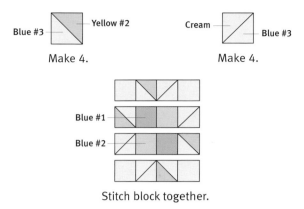

Make 4.   Make 4.

Blue #1
Blue #2

Stitch block together.

4. Make 1 Block C as shown. Press.

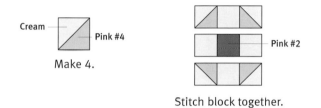

Cream — Pink #4
Make 4.

Pink #2

Stitch block together.

5. Make 14 half-square triangle units for the filler strips around Block 2. Press.

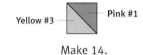

Yellow #3 — Pink #1
Make 14.

6. Make 9 half-square triangle units for the filler strip to the right of blocks A and 3. Press.

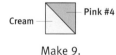

Cream — Pink #4
Make 9.

Appliqué
Appliqué blocks 1 through 12 and the corner squares, keeping appliqués out of the seam allowances.

Quilt Assembly

Refer to Block Names and Quilt Assembly Diagrams.

1. Arrange all the blocks so the 8" filler strips are below Block B, the 10" filler strips are below Block 5, and the 12" filler strips are below Block 1. The pink/yellow filler triangle units go around Block 2, and the pink/cream filler triangle units go to the right of Blocks A and 3.

2. Stitch the blocks and filler strips as shown in the Block Assembly Diagram. Stitch the units together. Press.

Border 1
1. Measure the length of the quilt. Cut the Border 1 strips to the measured length, and stitch to the sides of the quilt. Press. Measure the width of the quilt (including the side borders). Cut the Border 1 strips to the measured length, and stitch to the top and bottom of the quilt. Press.

Border 2
1. For Border 2, make strip sets as shown. Press.

2. Crosscut the strip sets into 2½" segments.

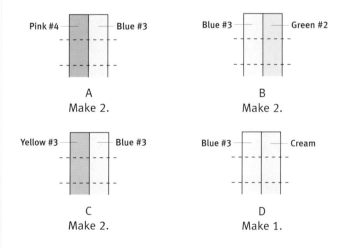

Pink #4 — Blue #3   Blue #3 — Green #2

A
Make 2.   B
Make 2.

Yellow #3 — Blue #3   Blue #3 — Cream

C
Make 2.   D
Make 1.

3. Make 2 side and 2 top/bottom borders as shown in the Quilt Assembly Diagram. Press.

4. Stitch the side borders to the quilt, adjusting the seams to fit if necessary. Press.

5. Stitch the corner squares to the top and bottom borders. Press. Stitch to the quilt, adjusting the seams to fit if necessary. Press.

Border 3

1. Measure the length of the quilt. Piece and cut the Border 3 strips to the measured length, and stitch to the sides of the quilt. Press. Measure the width of the quilt (including the side borders). Piece and cut the Border 3 strips to the measured length, and stitch to the top and bottom of the quilt. Press.

Finishing

1. Piece the backing so it is the same size as the batting. Layer and quilt as desired. Trim the backing and batting even with the quilt top.

2. Bind the quilt using a ³⁄₈" seam allowance. Refer to pages 109–110 for information on bindings.

Quilt Assembly Diagram

QUILT LABEL

Refer to page 19 for instructions on making quilt labels.

For:

From my heart to your home,
this quilt was stitched with love for you!

By:

Date:

Patterns are reversed for tracing to fusible web.

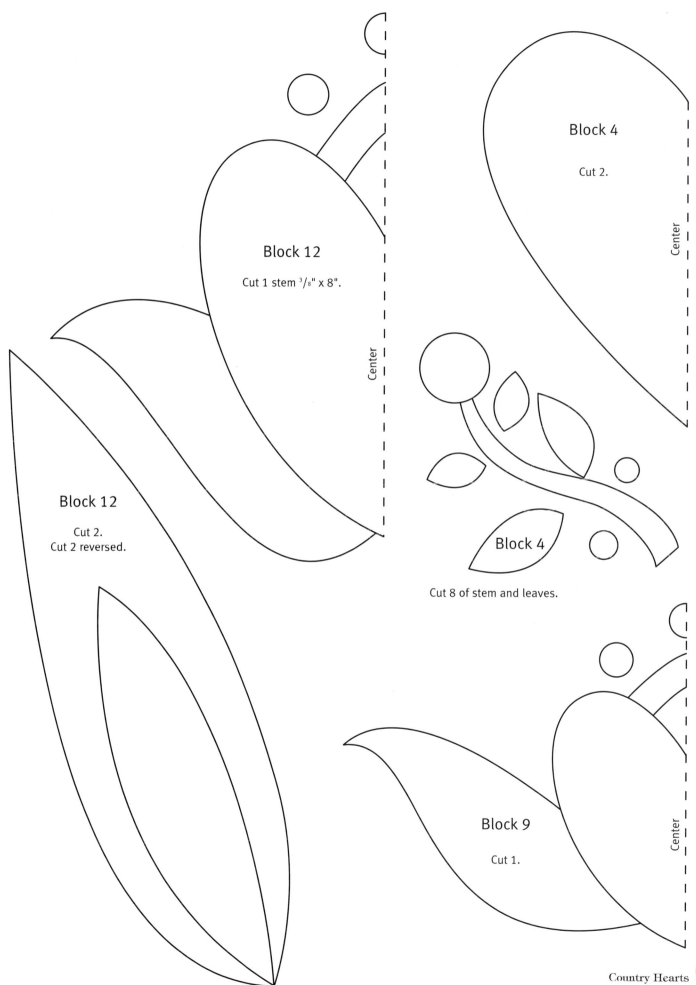

Block 4

Cut 2.

Center

Block 12

Cut 1 stem ³/₈" x 8".

Center

Block 4

Cut 8 of stem and leaves.

Block 12

Cut 2.
Cut 2 reversed.

Block 9

Cut 1.

Center

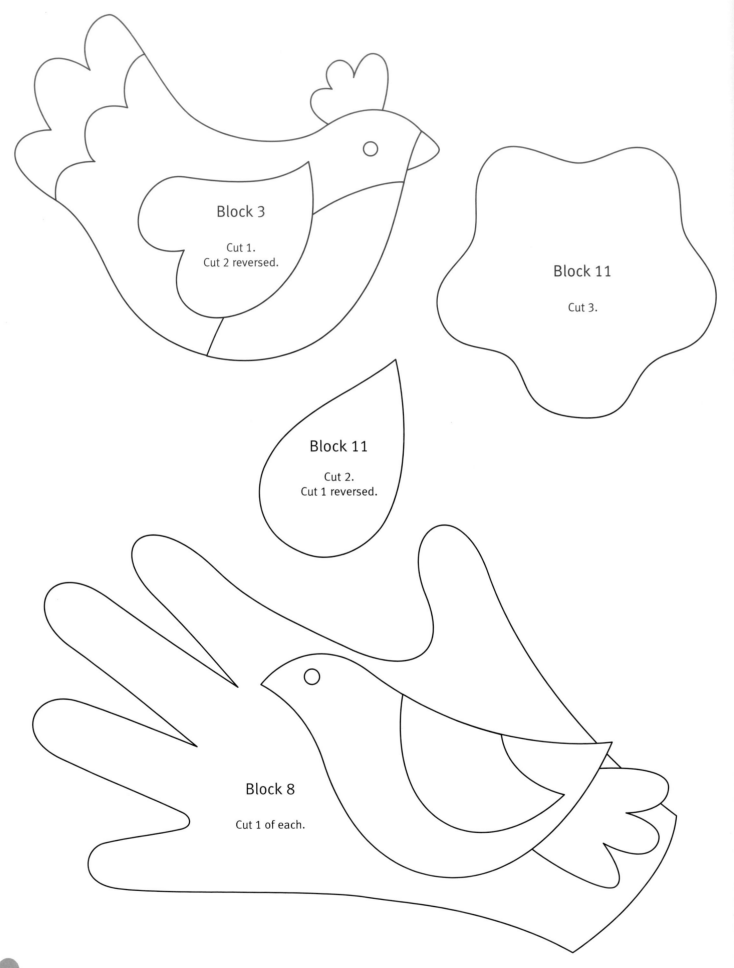

Block 3

Cut 1.
Cut 2 reversed.

Block 11

Cut 3.

Block 11

Cut 2.
Cut 1 reversed.

Block 8

Cut 1 of each.

Patterns are reversed for tracing to fusible web.

Block 2

Cut 1 of each.

Blocks 6 and 10 and Border 2 corners

Cut 6 of each.

Blocks 6 and 10

Cut 4.

Block 6

Cut 2.

Block 5

Cut 1 of each.

Match to dotted line on page 39 for full pattern.

Patterns are reversed for tracing to fusible web.

Block 1

Cut 1 of each.

Match to dotted line on page 38 for fLll pattern.

Block 5

Cut 1 of each.

Block 7

Cut 1 of each.

G·A·R·D·E·N S·O·N·G

Finished block size: 10" x 10"

MATERIALS AND YARDAGE

	Cradle	Crib	Twin
Finished quilt size	30" x 42"	46" x 58"	70" x 106"
Block sets	2 x 3	3 x 4	5 x 8
Total number of blocks	6	12	40
Muslin for blocks and sashing	1 ¼ yards	2 ¼ yards	5 ⅝ yards
Colored scraps to total	¾ yard	1 ½ yards	4 ½ yards
Green squares and triangles	½ yard	⅝ yard	2 yards
Striped border	1 ½ yards	2 ⅛ yards	3 ½ yards
Backing	1 ⅜ yards	3 ⅝ yards	6 ⅜ yards
Binding	⅜ yard	½ yard	¾ yard
Batting	36" x 48"	52" x 64"	76" x 112"

CUTTING

	Pattern/Cut Size	Cradle	Crib	Twin
Muslin				
Centers	C (page 45)	6	12	40
Diamonds	B (page 45)	48	96	320
Sashing strips	2 ½" x 10 ½"	17	31	93
Setting squares	2 ½" x 2 ½"	10	14	26
Scraps – petals	A (page 45)	48	96	320
Green fabric				
Block corner triangles	3 ⅞" x 3 ⅞"*	24	48	160
Setting squares	2 ½" x 2 ½"	2	6	28
Striped fabric				
Cut 2 lengthwise for the sides		2 ½" x 50"	4 ½" x 70"	4 ½" x 118"
Cut 2 lengthwise for top / bottom		2 ½" x 38"	4 ½" x 58"	4 ½" x 82"
Binding fabric				
Cut 2 ½" x width of the fabric		4 strips	6 strips	10 strips

* Cut squares in half diagonally.

DIRECTIONS

Refer to Quilting Basics (pages 102–110) as needed for quilt construction techniques. Use a ¼" seam allowance unless otherwise noted.

Block Assembly

Make the number of blocks you need for your selected quilt size.

1. Stitch the petals (A) together to form a circle. Press.

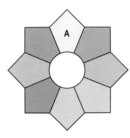

Stitch petals together.

2. Stitch the diamonds (B) to the block. Press.

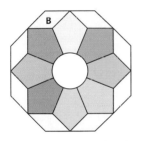

Stitch diamonds to block.

3. Stitch the corner triangles to the block. Press.

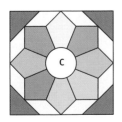

Stitch corner triangles.

4. Baste or iron the ¼" turn-under allowance on the center circle (C). Fold the circle into quarters and match to the seamlines. Appliqué the circle to the block. Press. Make the number of blocks you need for your selected quilt size.

Quilt Assembly

Refer to the Quilt Assembly Diagram.

1. Stitch the blocks and sashing strips into rows. Press.

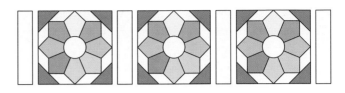

Stitch into rows.

2. Stitch the setting squares and sashing strips into rows. Be aware of color changes in the setting squares—all of the outside edge setting squares are muslin. Press.

Stitch into rows.

3. Stitch the rows together. Press.

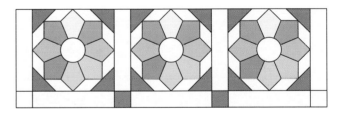

Stitch rows together.

Border

1. Stitch the borders to the quilt top. Refer to pages 106–107 for instructions on making mitered borders.

Finishing

1. Piece the backing so it is the same size as the batting. Layer and quilt as desired. Trim the backing and batting even with the quilt top.

2. Bind the quilt using a ³/₈" seam allowance. Refer to pages 109–110 for information on bindings.

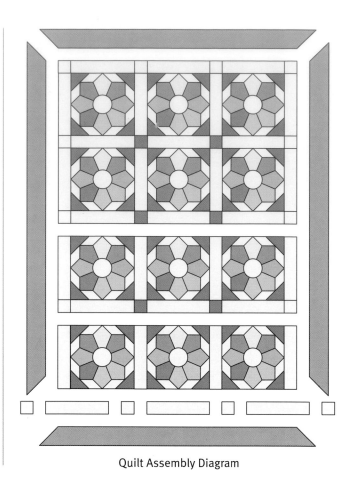

Quilt Assembly Diagram

GARDEN SONG TOY BLOCKS

No specific yardage is given since you can make the blocks using a different fabric for each side. If you choose, you can make the blocks larger or smaller to meet your needs.

MATERIALS AND YARDAGE

Blocks 30 squares 4 ¹/₂" x 4 ¹/₂"
Appliqué 5 squares 4 ¹/₂" x 4 ¹/₂" in colors that contrast with the fabrics for the blocks
Fusible web optional for fusible appliqué
Stuffing

DIRECTIONS

Use a ¹/₄" seam allowance unless otherwise noted.

1. Appliqué patterns are on page 46. Cut out the letters and heart and appliqué them onto 5 of the squares.

2. With right sides together, stitch 3 plain squares and 1 appliquéd square into a row. Start and stop stitching ¹/₄" from the edge of the fabric. Stitch the ends of the row together to form a loop.

3. With right sides together, stitch 1 square on to the top of the block, pivoting at each corner.

4. With right sides together, stitch the remaining square into the bottom of the block, pivoting at each corner. Leave one side open for turning.

5. Turn the block right side out, stuff, and slipstitch the opening closed.

6. Repeat to make 4 more blocks.

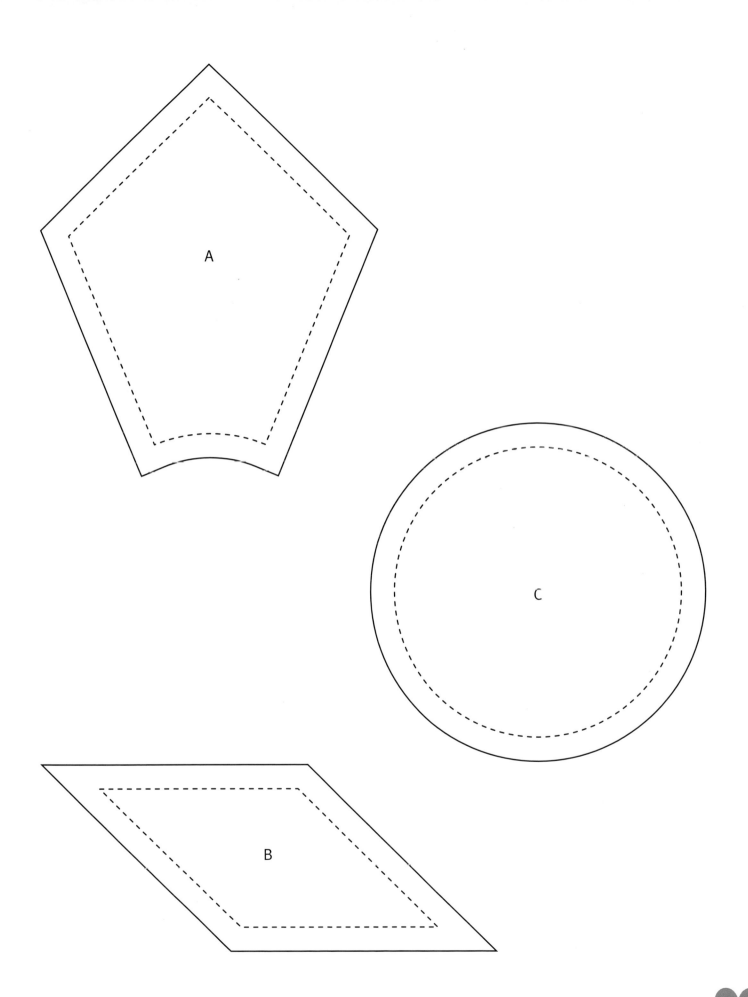

Photo by Diane Pedersen and Luke Mulks

Finished block size: 9" x 9"
Finished quilt size: 61" x 76"

MATERIALS AND YARDAGE

Fabric note: Choose pairs of bright pastels for each block (2 blues, 2 pinks, etc.).

Bright pastels $\frac{1}{3}$ yard each of 30 or more fabrics for blocks, half-blocks, Border 2, and binding

Greens $\frac{1}{4}$ yard each of 5 different greens for block centers and sashing squares

Light green 1 yard for sashing rectangles

White 2 yards for borders

Backing $4\frac{7}{8}$ yards

Batting 67" x 82"

CUTTING

NOTE: *The pieced border in this quilt requires exact piecing of all the elements, so exact lengths for all pieces of the quilt, except Border 3, are given in the cutting instructions.*

Bright pastel fabrics

For each block: Cut 4 squares $3\frac{1}{2}$" x $3\frac{1}{2}$" using 1 shade, and 4 squares $3\frac{1}{2}$" x $3\frac{1}{2}$" using the other shade of each color pair.

For each half-block: Cut 3 squares $3\frac{1}{2}$" x $3\frac{1}{2}$" using 1 shade, and 2 squares $3\frac{1}{2}$" x $3\frac{1}{2}$" using another shade of the same color.

Border 2: Cut 37 squares $3\frac{7}{8}$", then cut each in half diagonally.

Binding: Cut $2\frac{1}{2}$"-wide strips of varying lengths. You will need about 300" when pieced.

Green fabrics

Block centers: Cut 31 squares $3\frac{1}{2}$" x $3\frac{1}{2}$".

Sashing squares: Cut 32 squares 2" x 2".

Light green fabric

Sashing rectangles: Cut 48 rectangles 2" x $9\frac{1}{2}$".

White fabric

Border 1: Cut 6 strips $2\frac{1}{4}$" x width of the fabric; seam together end-to-end as needed, then cut into:
    2 pieces 60" long for the side borders
    2 pieces $48\frac{1}{2}$" long for the top and bottom borders.

Border 2: Cut 4 squares $3\frac{1}{2}$" x $3\frac{1}{2}$". Cut 37 squares $3\frac{7}{8}$" x $3\frac{7}{8}$", then cut each in half diagonally.

Border 3: Cut 7 strips 4" x width of the fabric.

DIRECTIONS

Refer to Quilting Basics (pages 102–110) as needed for quilt construction techniques. Use a $\frac{1}{4}$" seam allowance unless otherwise noted.

Block Assembly

1. Make 17 Nine-Patch blocks as shown. Press.

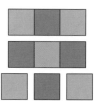

Stitch block together.   Make 17.

2. Make 14 half Nine-Patch blocks as shown. Press.

Stitch half-block together.   Make 14.

Quilt Assembly

Refer to the Quilt Assembly Diagram.

1. Arrange the blocks, half-blocks, sashing squares, and sashing rectangles.

2. Stitch the blocks and sashing rectangles into rows. Press.

3. Stitch the sashing squares and sashing rectangles into rows. Press.

4. Stitch the rows together. Press. Trim the outside edge of the quilt, leaving a $\frac{1}{4}$" seam allowance.

Border 1

1. Stitch the Border 1 side strips to the quilt top. Press. Stitch the Border 1 top and bottom strips to the quilt top. Press.

Border 2

1. Make 74 half-square triangle units as shown in the Quilt Assembly Diagram.

2. Stitch 21 half-square triangle units together for each side border.

3. Stitch the side borders to the quilt.

4. Stitch 16 half-square triangle units together for each of the top border and bottom borders. Stitch white squares to each end of the borders.

5. Stitch the top and bottom borders to the quilt. Press.

Border 3

1. Measure the length of the quilt. Piece and cut the Border 3 strips to the measured length, and stitch to the sides of the quilt. Measure the width of the quilt (including the side borders). Piece and cut the Border 3 strips to the measured length, and stitch to the top and bottom of the quilt. Press the seams toward the border.

Finishing

1. Piece the backing so it is the same size as the batting. Layer and quilt as desired. Trim the backing and batting even with the quilt top.

2. Bind the quilt using a $^3/_8$" seam allowance. Refer to pages 109–110 for information on bindings.

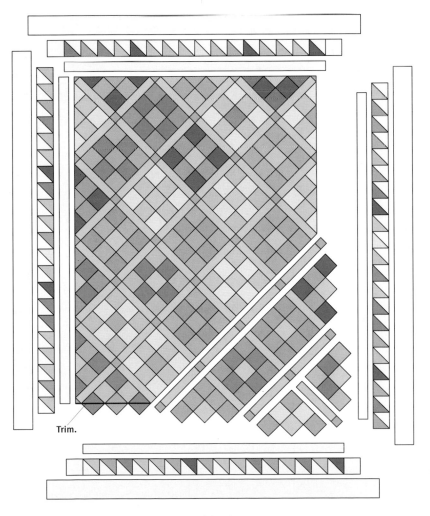

Trim.

Quilt Assembly Diagram

I·C·E C·R·Y·S·T·A·L·S

Finished block size: 10" x 10"
Finished quilt size: 86" x 106"

MATERIALS AND YARDAGE

Blue #1 (darkest) 3 ½ yards for Block A and Border 2
Blue #2 (dark) 1 yard for Block A and Block B
Blue #3 (darker medium) 2 ¼ yards for Block A, Border 1, and Border 3
Blue #4 (lighter medium) 1 ⅜ yards for Block A and Block B
Blue #5 (light) 3 ¾ yards for Block A, Block B, and Border 2
Fuchsia 1 ½ yards for Block A and Block B
White 2 ½ yards for Block B and Border 2 corners
Backing 8 yards
Binding ⅞ yard
Batting 92" x 112"

CUTTING

This quilt can be made using the Easy Triangles technique for the half-square triangle units. Using this method, you will have a few units left over. For the Easy Triangle method, you will need 138 copies of page 100. Alternate cutting directions are given if you prefer not to use Easy Triangles.

NOTE: *The pieced border in this quilt requires exact piecing of all the elements, so exact lengths for all pieces of the quilt, except Border 3, are given in the cutting instructions.*

Blue #1 fabric

Block A: Cut either 64 squares 6 ½" x 6 ½" for Easy Triangles **or** cut 256 squares 2 ⅞" x 2 ⅞", then cut each in half diagonally.
Border 2: Cut either 43 squares 6 ½" x 6 ½" for Easy Triangles **or** cut 172 squares 2 ⅞" x 2 ⅞", then cut each in half diagonally.

Blue #2 fabric

Block A: Cut 128 squares 2 ½" x 2 ½".
Block B: Cut 31 squares 2 ½" x 2 ½".

Blue #3 fabric

Block A: Cut either 16 squares 6 ½" x 6 ½" for Easy Triangles **or** cut 64 squares 2 ⅞" x 2 ⅞", then cut each in half diagonally.
Border 1: Cut 9 strips 2 ½" x width of the fabric; seam together end-to-end, then cut into:
    2 pieces 90 ½" long for the side borders
    2 pieces 74 ½" long for the top and bottom borders.
Border 3: Cut 11 strips 2 ½" x width of the fabric.

Blue #4 fabric

Block A: Cut 128 squares 2 ½" x 2 ½".
Block B: Cut 124 squares 2 ½" x 2 ½".

Blue #5 fabric

Block A: Cut either 48 squares 6 ½" x 6 ½" for Easy Triangles **or** cut 192 squares 2 ⅞" x 2 ⅞", then cut each in half diagonally.
Block B: Cut 124 squares 2 ½" x 2 ½".
Border 2: Cut either 43 squares 6 ½" x 6 ½" for Easy Triangles **or** cut 172 squares 2 ⅞" x 2 ⅞", then cut each in half diagonally.

Fuchsia fabric

Block A: Cut 32 squares 2 ½" x 2 ½".
Block B: Cut either 31 squares 6 ½" x 6 ½" for Easy Triangles **or** cut 124 squares 2 ⅞" x 2 ⅞", then cut each in half diagonally.

White fabric

Block B: Cut 248 squares 2 ½" x 2 ½". Cut either 31 squares 6 ½" x 6 ½" for Easy Triangles **or** cut 124 squares 2 ⅞" x 2 ⅞", then cut each in half diagonally.
Border 2 corners: Cut 8 squares 2 ½" x 2 ½".

Binding fabric

Cut 10 strips 2 ½" x the width of the fabric.

DIRECTIONS

Refer to Quilting Basics (pages 102–110) as needed for quilt construction techniques. Use a ¹/₄" seam allowance unless otherwise noted.

Block Assembly

Block A

1. Make 384 half-square triangle units using the #1 and #5 blue fabrics, and make 128 half-square triangle units using the #1 and #3 blue fabrics. Use the 2" Finished Easy Triangles (refer to page 100), or piece together triangles cut from the 2⁷/₈" squares.

Blue #1 — Blue #5

Make 384.

Blue #1 — Blue #3

Make 128.

2. Make 32 Block A as shown.

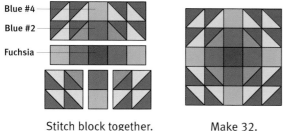

Stitch block together.   Make 32.

Block B

1. Make 248 half-square triangle units using the fuchsia and white fabrics. Use the 2" Finished Easy Triangles (refer to page 100), or piece together triangles cut from the 2⁷/₈" squares.

Make 248.

2. Make 31 Block B as shown.

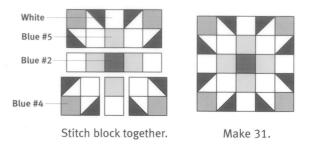

Stitch block together.   Make 31.

Quilt Assembly

Refer to the Quilt Assembly Diagram.

1. Stitch the blocks together into rows, alternating the A and B blocks. Press the seam allowances in alternate directions for each row, so the seams nest when the rows are stitched together.

2. Stitch the rows together. Press.

Border 1

1. Stitch the Border 1 side strips to the quilt top. Press. Stitch the Border 1 top and bottom strips to the quilt top. Press.

Border 2

1. Make 344 half-square triangle units using the #1 and #5 blue fabrics. Use the 2" Finished Easy Triangles (refer to page 100), or piece together triangles cut from the 2⁷/₈" squares.

Make 344.

2. Stitch the units into border sections as shown in the Quilt Assembly Diagram. Press.

3. Stitch the side borders to the quilt. Press.

4. Stitch the top and bottom borders to the quilt. Press.

Border 3

1. Measure the length of the quilt. Piece and cut the Border 3 strips to the measured length, and stitch to the sides of quilt. Press. Measure the width of the quilt (including the side borders). Piece and cut the Border 3 strips to the measured length, and stitch to the top and bottom of the quilt. Press.

Finishing

1. Piece the backing so it is the same size as the batting. Layer and quilt as desired. Trim the backing and batting even with the quilt top.

2. Bind the quilt using a ³/₈" seam allowance. Refer to pages 109–110 for information on bindings.

Quilt Assembly Diagram

IN THE MEADOW WE CAN
B·U·I·L·D A S·N·O·W·M·A·N

Finished quilt size: 51" x 63"

MATERIALS AND YARDAGE

Refer to Block Names Diagram on page 56 for quilt section numbers.

Plaids and prints 1 ⅝ yards for snowman background (1) and 1 ⅝ yards for lettering at right (2) and top (3)
See Cutting below for other background yardage requirements.
White print ½ yard for snowman bottom section and head appliqué
Red print #1 ¾ yard for snowman coat appliqué
Red print #2 ⅓ yard for stocking cap appliqué
Plaid #1 ½ yard for snowman scarf appliqué
Plaid #2 ⅜ yard for snowman hat appliqué
Plaid #3 ¼ yard for lettering appliqué
A variety of scraps for other appliqués—refer to patterns on pages 58–61 for sizes
Black print ⅜ yard for Border 1
Plaid #4 ¾ yard for Border 2
Backing 3 ½ yards
Binding ½ yard
Batting 57" x 69"
Buttons 2 buttons 1 ¼" for eyes, 5 buttons ¾" for mouth, 3 buttons 1" for coat, 10 buttons ½" for boots
Fusible web (optional for fusible appliqué)

CUTTING

Note: Dimensions of the backgrounds are given width first to clarify how they fit into the quilt layout.

Background fabrics

1 – Snowman: Cut 1 rectangle 17 ½" x 54 ½".
2 – Lettering at right: Cut 1 rectangle 3 ½" x 54 ½".
3 – Lettering at top: Cut 1 rectangle 22 ½" x 3 ½".
4 – Left snowflake: Cut 1 rectangle 11 ½" x 9 ½".
5 – Right snowflake: Cut 1 rectangle 11 ½" x 9 ½".
6 – Stocking cap: Cut 1 rectangle 11 ½" x 8 ½".
7 – Scarf: Cut 1 rectangle 11 ½" x 8 ½".
8 – Mittens: Cut 1 rectangle 11 ½" x 9 ½".
9 – Scarf: Cut 1 rectangle 11 ½" x 9 ½".

Background fabrics (continued)

10 – Tree: Cut 1 rectangle 8 ½" x 14 ½".
11 – Tip of pipe: Cut 1 rectangle 3 ½" x 4 ½".
12 – Tip of carrot: Cut 1 rectangle 3 ½" x 4 ½".
13 – Heart: Cut 1 rectangle 3 ½" x 6 ½".
14 – Right-facing boot: Cut 1 square 11 ½" x 11 ½".
15 – Pipe: Cut 1 rectangle 11 ½" x 4 ½".
16 – Carrot: Cut 1 rectangle 11 ½" x 4 ½".
17 – Left-facing boot: Cut 1 rectangle 11 ½" x 12 ½".
18 – Star: Cut 1 square 5 ½" x 5 ½".
19 – Mug: Cut 1 rectangle 6 ½" x 5 ½".

Appliqué fabrics

Snowman bottom section: Cut 1 rectangle 17 ¼" x 10 ¼".
Snowman coat: Cut 1 rectangle 19 ½" x 29".
Snowman top scarf: Cut 1 rectangle 13 ½" x 7".
Snowman bottom scarf: Cut 1 rectangle 15" x 6 ½".
Snowman sleeves. Cut 2 squares 6" x 6".
Snowman patches: Cut 2 squares 6 ½" x 6 ½".
Snowflakes: Cut 1 square 11" x 11" and 1 square 6" x 6".
All other appliqués: refer to patterns on pages 58–61.

Black print fabric

Border 1: Cut 5 strips 2" x width of the fabric.

Plaid #4 fabric

Border 2: Cut 6 strips 3 ½" x width of the fabric.

Binding fabric

Cut 6 strips 2 ½" x width of the fabric.

DIRECTIONS

Refer to Quilting Basics (pages 102–110) as needed for quilt construction techniques. Use a ¼" seam allowance unless otherwise noted.

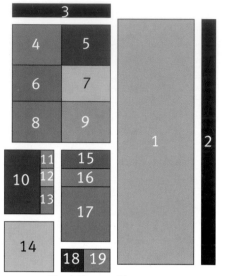

Block Names Diagram

Snowflake Pattern

1. Fold an 11" square of paper in half, in half again.

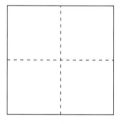

Fold in halves.

2. Fold in thirds as shown. Reduce the bulk by making the last 2 folds accordion-style, ⅓ in one direction and ⅓ in the other direction.

Fold in thirds.

3. Make a mark (such as an "x") on the outside segment, and open up the paper.

4. Place the marked segment over the large snowflake pattern on page 60, lining up the dotted line on the folds. Trace the solid lines.

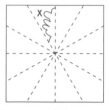

Trace snowflake pattern.

5. Refold with the tracing on the outside, and cut out on the line.

Refold and cut.

6. Use this pattern to cut out the large snowflake.

Complete snowflake pattern

7. Repeat with the 6" square and the small snowflake pattern.

Quilt Assembly

Refer to the Block Names and Quilt Assembly Diagrams.

1. For ease in handling, appliqué the blocks that do not overlap other blocks first: Blocks 2, 3, 5, 8, 10, 13, 14, and 19.

2. Stitch the backgrounds together following the diagram, except for #2. It will be stitched to the quilt later, catching the snowman bottom section and coat in the seam. The dimensions of the backgrounds in the Cutting section are given width first to clarify how they fit into the quilt layout.

3. The illustrations below are for the finished-size snowman bottom, coat, and scarf pieces. Work from the right side of the fabric when cutting down the rectangles to these shapes. Add a turn-under allowance if you are doing hand appliqué.

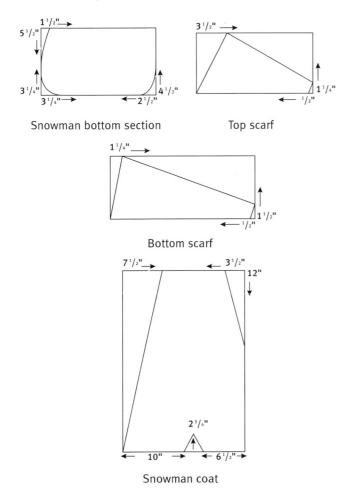

Snowman bottom section

Top scarf

Bottom scarf

Snowman coat

4. Line up the right and bottom raw edges of the snowman bottom section with the right and bottom raw edges of the snowman background. Line up the right raw edge of the coat with the right raw edge of the snowman background. After positioning the snowman's left sleeve, trim it even with the right edge of the snowman background.

5. Finish the appliqués. Stitch the lettering panel (2) to the quilt.

Borders

1. Measure the length of the quilt. Piece and cut the Border 1 strips to the measured length, and stitch to the sides of the quilt. Press. Measure the width of the quilt (including the side borders). Piece and cut the Border 1 strips to the measured length, and stitch to the top and bottom of the quilt. Press.

2. Measure the length of the quilt. Piece and cut the Border 2 strips to the measured length, and stitch to the sides of the quilt. Press. Measure the width of the quilt (including the side borders). Piece and cut the Border 2 strips to the measured length, and stitch to the top and bottom of the quilt. Press.

Finishing

1. Piece the backing so it is the same size as the batting. Layer and quilt as desired. Trim the backing and batting even with the quilt top.

2. Bind the quilt using a $\frac{3}{8}$" seam allowance. Refer to pages 109–110 for information on bindings.

3. Sew buttons to the quilt for the eyes and mouth, and on the coat and boots.

Quilt Assembly Diagram

Patterns are reversed for tracing to fusible web. Enlarge patterns 200%.

Add bird eye with permanent marker.

Reverse for second mitten.

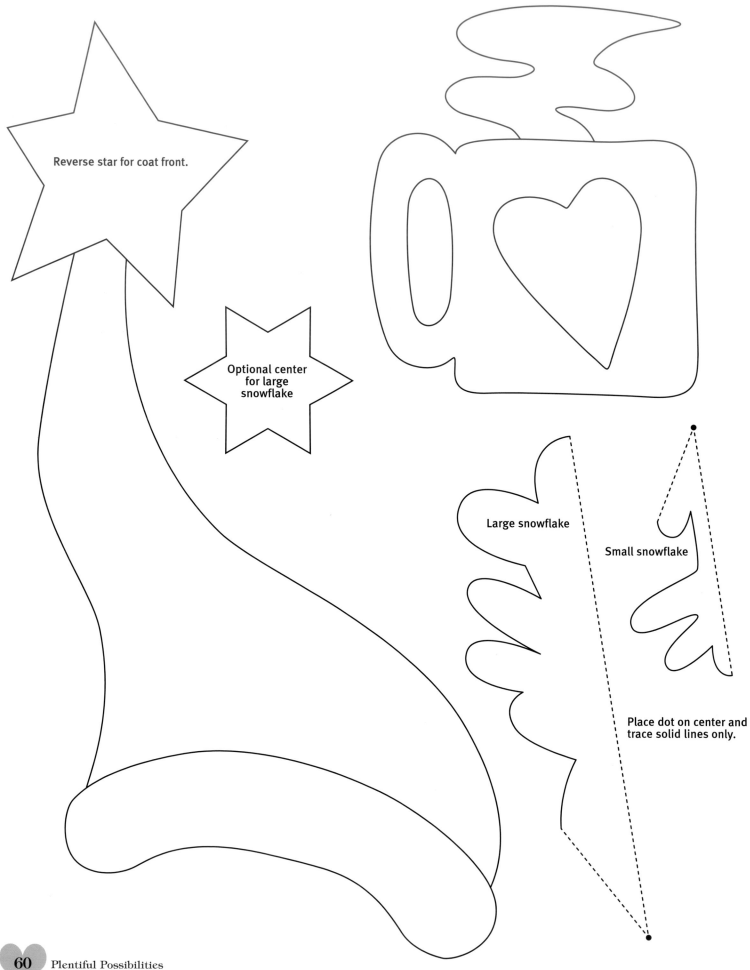

Reverse star for coat front.

Optional center for large snowflake

Large snowflake

Small snowflake

Place dot on center and trace solid lines only.

Patterns are reversed for tracing to fusible web. Enlarge patterns 200%.

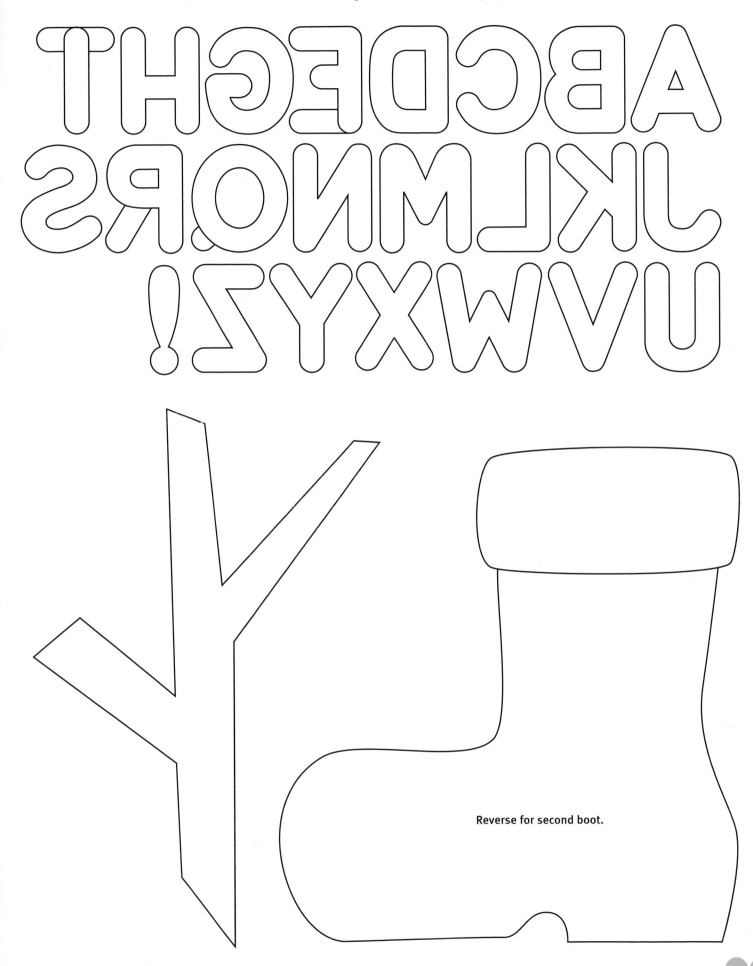

Reverse for second boot.

I S·P·Y N·A·P·P·I·N·G Q·U·I·L·T

Finished hexagon width: 3 1/8"
Finished quilt size: 47" x 53"

MATERIALS AND YARDAGE

Conversation prints A wide variety of pieces at least
  4" square, to total 2 1/2 yards for hexagons
Red 1 3/4 yards for triangles and Border 2
Black 3/8 yard for Border 1
Backing 3 1/8 yards
Binding 1/2 yard
Batting 53" x 59"

CUTTING

Patterns are on page 64.

Conversation print fabrics
Hexagons: Cut 200 using pattern A.

Red fabric
Triangles: Cut 400 using pattern B.
Border 2: Cut 6 strips 3 1/2" x width of the fabric.

Black fabric
Border 1: Cut 5 strips 2" x width of the fabric.

Binding fabric
Cut 6 strips 2 1/2" x width of the fabric.

DIRECTIONS

*Refer to Quilting Basics (pages 102–110) as needed for
quilt construction techniques. Use a 1/4" seam allowance unless
otherwise noted.*

Quilt Assembly

Refer to the Quilt Assembly Diagram.

1. Stitch the hexagons and triangles into rows, as
shown. Odd rows have 13 hexagons and begin and
end with hexagons. Even rows have 12 hexagons and
begin and end with triangles.

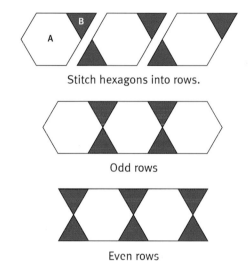

Stitch hexagons into rows.

Odd rows

Even rows

2. Press all seams in odd rows to the right, and all
seams in even rows to the left.

3. Stitch the rows together. Press well.

4. Trim the sides to straighten the edges.

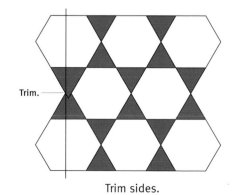

Trim.

Trim sides.

Borders

1. Measure the width of the quilt. Piece and cut the Border 1 strips to the measured length, and stitch to the top and bottom of the quilt. Press. Measure the length of the quilt (including the top and bottom borders). Piece and cut the Border 1 strips to the measured length, and stitch to the sides of the quilt. Press.

2. Measure the width of the quilt. Piece and cut the Border 2 strips to the measured length, and stitch to the top and bottom of the quilt. Press. Measure the length of the quilt (including the top and bottom borders). Piece and cut the Border 2 strips to the measured length, and stitch to the sides of the quilt. Press.

3. On Border 1, hand or machine embroider the names of items children can find in the hexagons.

Finishing

1. Piece the backing so it is the same size as the batting. Layer and quilt as desired. Trim the backing and batting even with the quilt top.

2. Bind the quilt using a ³/₈" seam allowance. Refer to pages 109–110 for information on bindings.

Quilt Assembly Diagram

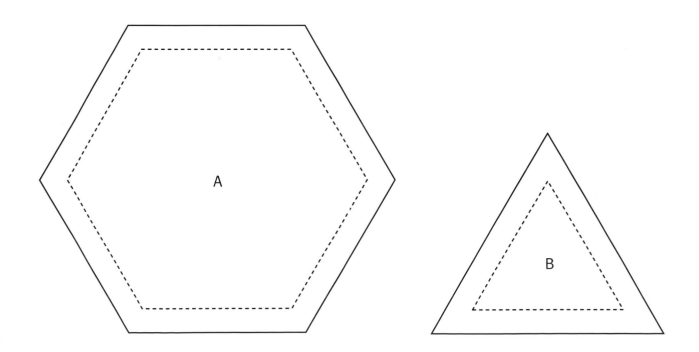

Finished quilt size: 85" x 85"

MATERIALS AND YARDAGE

Black 2 3/8 yards for Nine-Patch blocks, alternate squares, and Border 3

Purple 2 3/8 yards for Nine-Patch blocks and large setting triangles

Teal 1 1/4 yards for Nine-Patch blocks and Border 2

Brick red 1 3/8 yards for Nine-Patch blocks, alternate squares, and Border 3

Olive 5/8 yard for Nine-Patch blocks and Border 1

Gold 1/2 yard for Nine-Patch blocks, Border 1 squares, and Border 3 squares

Rust 1/4 yard for alternate squares and Border 2 squares

Backing 7 7/8 yards

Binding 3/4 yard

Batting 91" x 91"

CUTTING

Black fabric
Nine-Patch blocks: Cut 1 strip 2" x width of the fabric.
Alternate squares: Cut 5 squares 14" x 14".
Border 3: Cut 4 strips 7 1/2" x width of the fabric.

Purple fabric
Nine-Patch blocks: Cut 4 strips 2" x width of the fabric.
Setting triangles: Cut 2 squares 33 3/4" x 33 3/4", then cut each in half diagonally.

Teal fabric
Nine-Patch blocks: Cut 4 strips 2" x width of the fabric.
Border 2: Cut 8 strips 3 1/2" x width of the fabric.

Brick red fabric
Nine-Patch blocks: Cut 1 strip 2" x width of the fabric.
Alternate squares: Cut 16 squares 5" x 5".
Border 3: Cut 4 strips 7 1/2" x width of the fabric.

Olive fabric
Nine-Patch blocks: Cut 1 strip 2" x width of the fabric.
Border 1: Cut 4 strips 3 1/2" x width of the fabric.

Gold fabric
Nine-Patch blocks: Cut 1 strip 2" x width of the fabric.
Border 1: Cut 4 squares 3 1/2" x 3 1/2".
Border 3: Cut 4 squares 7 1/2" x 7 1/2".

Rust fabric
Alternate squares: Cut 4 squares 5" x 5".
Border 2: Cut 4 squares 3 1/2" x 3 1/2".

Binding fabric
Binding: Cut 9 strips 2 1/2" x width of the fabric.

DIRECTIONS

Refer to Quilting Basics (pages 102–110) as needed for quilt construction techniques. Use a 1/4" seam allowance unless otherwise noted.

Block Assembly

1. Make 2 strip sets using the purple and teal strips as shown. Press.

Make 2.

2. Cut the remaining strips for the Nine-Patch blocks into 4 segments of approximately 10" each. Make a 10" strip set with teal strips on each side and black in the center. Repeat with gold, brick, and olive centers. Press.

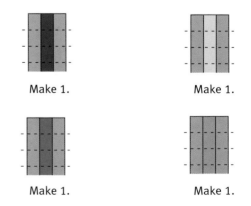

Make 1. Make 1.

Make 1. Make 1.

3. Crosscut all strip sets into 2" segments.

4. Make 4 Nine-Patch blocks with black centers, 4 with gold centers, 4 with brick centers, and 4 with olive centers. Press.

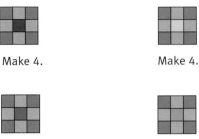

Make 4. Make 4.

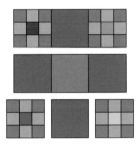

Make 4. Make 4.

Quilt Assembly

Refer to the Quilt Assembly Diagram.

1. Stitch the Nine-Patch blocks, the 5" brick red squares, and the 5" rust squares into 3 rows, as shown. Press the seam allowances in alternate directions for each row, so the seams nest when the rows are stitched together. Stitch the rows together to form larger Nine-Patch blocks. Press.

Stitch block together. Make 4.

2. Stitch the blocks from Step 1 and the 14" black squares into 3 rows, as shown. Stitch the rows together. Press.

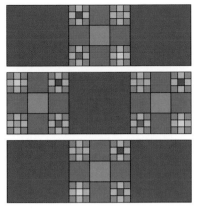

Stitch rows together.

Border 1

1. Measure the width of the quilt. Cut 4 Border 1 strips to the measured length. Stitch the side borders to the quilt. Press. Stitch the 3 ½" gold squares to each end of the remaining Border 1 strips and stitch the strips to the top and bottom of the quilt. Press.

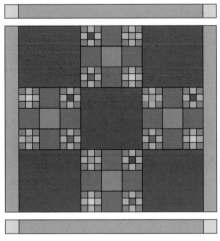

Add Border 1.

2. Stitch 1 purple setting triangle to each side of the quilt. Press.

Border 2

1. Measure the width of the quilt. Piece together and cut 4 Border 2 strips to the measured length. Stitch the side borders to the quilt. Press. Stitch the 3 ½" rust squares to each end of the remaining two Border 2 strips, and stitch the strips to the top and bottom of the quilt. Press.

Border 3

1. Measure the width of the quilt. Piece together and cut 2 Border 3 black strips and 2 Border 3 brick strips to the measured length. Stitch the side borders to the quilt. Press. Stitch the 7 1/2" gold squares to each end of the remaining 2 Border 3 strips, and stitch the strips to the top and bottom of the quilt. Press.

Finishing

1. Piece the backing so it is the same size as the batting. Layer and quilt as desired. Trim the backing and batting even with the quilt top.

2. Bind the quilt using a 3/8" seam allowance. Refer to pages 109–110 for information on bindings.

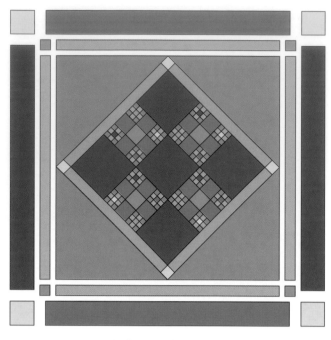

Quilt Assembly Diagram

NOT QUITE AMISH PILLOW

Finished size: 20" x 20"

MATERIALS AND YARDAGE

Black 1 1/8 yards for Nine-Patch blocks, border, and pillow back
Purple 1/8 yard for Nine-Patch blocks
Teal 1/8 yard for Nine-Patch blocks
Brick red 1/4 yard for Nine-Patch blocks and alternate squares
Gold 1/4 yard for Nine-Patch blocks and border squares
Pillow form 20" x 20"

CUTTING

Black fabric
Nine-Patch blocks: Cut 2 squares 2" x 2".
Border: Cut 2 strips 3 1/4" x width of the fabric.
Backing: Cut 2 rectangles 19 1/2" x 28".

Purple fabric
Nine-Patch blocks: Cut 20 squares 2" x 2".

Teal fabric
Nine-Patch blocks: Cut 20 squares 2" x 2".

Brick red fabric
Nine-Patch block: Cut 1 square 2" x 2".
Alternate squares: Cut 4 squares 5" x 5".

Gold fabric
Nine-Patch blocks: Cut 2 squares 2" x 2".
Border: Cut 4 squares 3 1/4" x 3 1/4".

DIRECTIONS

Use a ¼" seam allowance unless otherwise noted.

Block Assembly

1. Sew the 2" squares together to make 5 Nine-Patch blocks as shown. Press.

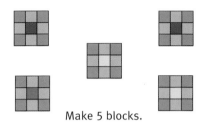

Make 5 blocks.

2. Stitch the Nine-Patch blocks and alternate squares into 3 rows, as shown. Press.

3. Stitch the rows together. Press the pillow top.

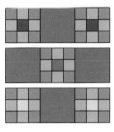

Stitch rows together.

Pillow Assembly

1. Measure the width of the pillow top. From the black border strips, cut 4 strips to the measured length and stitch 2 of the strips to opposite sides of the pillow top. Press. Stitch the 3¼" gold squares to the ends of the remaining 2 black border strips. Stitch the strips to other sides of the pillow top. Press.

2. Make the envelope back by pressing each pillow back piece in half, wrong sides together. When folded, each will measure 19½" x 14". Place both pieces on the right side of the pillow top, matching raw edges and overlapping the folded edges in the center. Pin in place.

3. Stitch around the entire outside edge of the pillow. Clip the corners and turn right side out. Press. Insert the pillow form.

QUILT LABEL

Refer to page 19 for instructions on making quilt labels.

To:

Made by:

Date:

P·A·T·H T·H·R·O·U·G·H T·H·E P·I·N·E·S

Finished block size: 12" x 12"
Finished quilt size: 84" x 108"

Use traditional templates to make this block or try your hand at paper piecing. Refer to pages 104–105 for information on paper piecing.

MATERIALS AND YARDAGE

Light brown print 5 ½ yards for background
Green print 1 ¾ yards for trees
Brown ¼ yard for tree trunks
Yellow 2 ½ yards for stars
Red 1 yard for Four-Patch blocks
Brown print 3 yards for border
Backing 7 ¾ yards
Binding ⅞ yard
Batting 90" x 114"

CUTTING

Patterns are on pages 76–77.

Light brown print
Tree background: Cut 17 of each using patterns A, B, and C. Cut 17 of each using patterns A, B, and C reversed.
Tree trunk background: Cut 4 strips 5 ¾" x width of the fabric.
Star background: Cut 88 using pattern G *or* use the paper-piecing pattern.
Four-Patch blocks: Cut 11 strips 2 ½" x width of the fabric.

Green print
Trees: Cut 17 of each using patterns D, E, and F.

Brown fabric
Tree trunks: Cut 2 strips 2" x width of the fabric.

Yellow fabric
Star center squares: Cut 22 squares 4 ½" x 4 ½".
Star points: Cut 88 using pattern H and 88 using pattern H reversed *or* use the paper-piecing pattern.

Red fabric
Four-Patch blocks: Cut 11 strips 2 ½" x width of the fabric.

Brown print fabric
Border: Cut 8 strips 12 ½" x width of the fabric.

Binding fabric
Cut 11 strips 2 ¼" x width of the fabric.

DIRECTIONS

Refer to Quilting Basics (pages 102–110) as needed for quilt construction techniques. Use a ¼" seam allowance unless otherwise noted.

Block Assembly

Tree Blocks
1. Make two strip sets for the trunk using the tree trunk strips and the 5 ¾" background strips. Press. Crosscut into 17 segments 3 ½" wide.

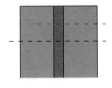

Make 2.

2. Make 17 of each tree block as shown. Press.

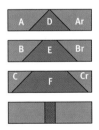 

Stitch block together.   Make 17.

Star Blocks
Four-Patch Blocks
1. Make 11 strip sets for the Four-Patch blocks by stitching a 2 ½" background strip to a 2 ½" red fabric strip. Press.

2. Crosscut the strip sets into 176 segments 2 ½" wide.

3. Stitch pairs of segments together as shown to make 88 Four-Patch blocks. Press.

Stitch segments together.   Make 88.

Star Block Assembly

1. Make 88 star point units using pieces cut from patterns G and H, or by using the optional paper-piecing pattern on page 77. Press.

Make 88.

2. Assemble the Four-Patch blocks and star point units into 22 blocks as shown. Press.

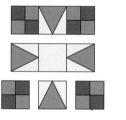

Stitch block together.   Make 22.

Quilt Assembly

Refer to the Quilt Assembly Diagram.

1. Stitch the blocks into rows, alternating the star and tree blocks. Press the seam allowances in alternate directions for each row, so the seams nest when the rows are stitched together.

2. Stitch the rows together. Press.

Borders

1. Measure the length and width of the quilt. Piece and cut the border strips to the measured lengths. Stitch the side borders to the sides of the quilt.Press. Stitch the remaining star blocks to the ends of the top and bottom borders, and stitch to the quilt. Press.

Finishing

1. Piece the backing so it is the same size as the batting. Layer and quilt as desired. Trim the backing and batting even with the quilt top.

2. Bind the quilt using a $1/4$" seam allowance. Refer to pages 109–110 for information on bindings.

Quilt Assembly Diagram

PATH THROUGH THE PINES VALANCE

Finished block size: 12" x 12"
Height: 17", width is adjustable

For best results, the heading and lining fabric should be the same fabric as the block background.

MATERIALS AND YARDAGE

To determine the number of blocks to make:
Measure the width of the window and multiply by two. Divide the answer by twelve and round up to the nearest number.
Example: Window width = 71"

$$71" \times 2 = 142"$$
$$142" \div 12 = 11.8"$$

Round up to 12 blocks.

To determine the block yardage:
1. Each tree block takes $1/8$ yard each of green and light brown, and a 2" x 3$1/2$" piece of dark brown.

2. Figure the required yardage based on the number of tree blocks. For example, 12 tree blocks would take 1$1/2$ yards of green and $1/6$ yard of dark brown. The light brown block background yardage is included in the heading/lining yardage.

To determine the heading/lining yardage:
1. Multiply the number of blocks for the width of the valance as determined above by 12". For example, for twelve tree blocks: 12 blocks x 12" = 144" = 4 yards. Add $1/4$ yard for shrinkage and seam allowances, for a total of 4$1/4$ yards.

2. Cut off a piece 22$1/2$" x the length of the fabric for the heading/lining and set it aside, then use the remaining long narrow piece of fabric for cutting out the background for the blocks.

DIRECTIONS

Use a $1/4$" seam allowance unless otherwise noted.

1. Make the tree blocks using the directions on page 71. There is considerable waste in making two strip sets for the tree trunk units, so it is advisable to cut each needed trunk 2" x 3$1/2$" and the background pieces for each side of the trunk 5$3/4$" x 3$1/2$", then piece each tree trunk unit individually. Press each block.

2. Stitch the blocks together in a row. Press.

3. Use the 22$1/2$" length of background fabric for the heading/lining. Stitch one long side of the heading/lining to the bottom of the block row, right sides together. Stitch the other side to the top of the block row, right sides together, forming a tube. Press.

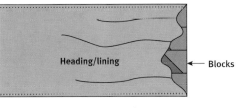

Heading/lining ← Blocks

Stitch to form a tube.

4. Press and then stitch a $1/4$" hem to the wrong side on both open ends of the valance.

5. Turn right side out. Press the valance so the bottom edge of the tree blocks forms the bottom edge of the valance.

6. To make the casing: Measure up 3" from the top of the tree blocks and draw a line the full width of the valance. Stitch on the line and in the seam at the top of the tree blocks.

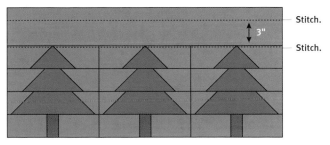

Stitch.
↕ 3"
Stitch.

Make casing.

FRIENDSHIP PILLOWS

❖ ❖

Finished size: 10" x 11"

These sweet little pillows are made with scraps and imagination. See Cutting to determine yardage requirements.

CUTTING

Background fabric Cut 1 rectangle 6 1/2" x 7 1/2".
Border 1 fabrics Cut 4 rectangles 1 1/2" x 12".
Border 2 fabrics Cut 4 rectangles 1 1/2" x 12".
Back fabric Cut 1 rectangle 10 1/2" x 11 1/2".

DIRECTIONS

Use a 1/4" seam allowance unless otherwise noted.
Patterns are on pages 78–80.

1. Enlarge your chosen pattern 120% on a photocopier.

2. Appliqué using your preferred method. Trace the lettering and other details onto the block with a permanent marking pen, or embroider. **Note that these patterns are not reversed for fusible web appliqué.**

3. Add Borders 1 and 2 by stitching the strips to the block and trimming off any excess. Press.

4. If you like, embellish with buttons sewn on with six strands of embroidery floss.

5. Pin the pillow top and back with right sides together. Stitch around the edges leaving a 4" opening for stuffing. Trim the corners, turn right side out, and stuff. Slipstitch the opening closed.

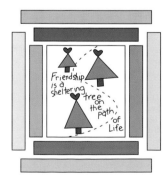

Pillow Assembly Diagram

FRIENDSHIP WALLHANGINGS

❖ ❖

Finished size: 15" x 17"

These little wallhangings are made with scraps and imagination. See Cutting to determine yardage requirements.

CUTTING

Background fabric Cut 1 rectangle 7 1/2" x 9 1/2".
Border 1 fabrics Cut 4 rectangles 1 1/2" x 12".
Border 2 fabrics Cut 4 rectangles 3 1/2" x 18".
Backing fabric Cut 1 rectangle 17" x 19".
Binding fabric Cut 2 strips 2 1/2" x width of the fabric.
Batting 17" x 19"

DIRECTIONS

Use a 1/4" seam allowance unless otherwise noted.
Patterns are on pages 78–80.

1. Enlarge your chosen pattern 140% on a photocopier.

2. Appliqué using your preferred method. Trace the lettering and other details onto the block with a permanent pen, or embroider. **Note that these patterns are not reversed for fusible web appliqué.**

3. Add Borders 1 and 2 by stitching the strips to the block and trimming off any excess. Press.

4. If you like, embellish with buttons sewn on with six strands of embroidery floss.

Finishing

1. Layer and quilt as desired. Trim the backing and batting even with the wallhanging top.

2. Bind the wallhanging using a ⅜" seam allowance. Refer to pages 109–110 for information on bindings.

Wallhanging Assembly Diagram

QUILT LABEL

Refer to page 19 for instructions on making quilt labels.

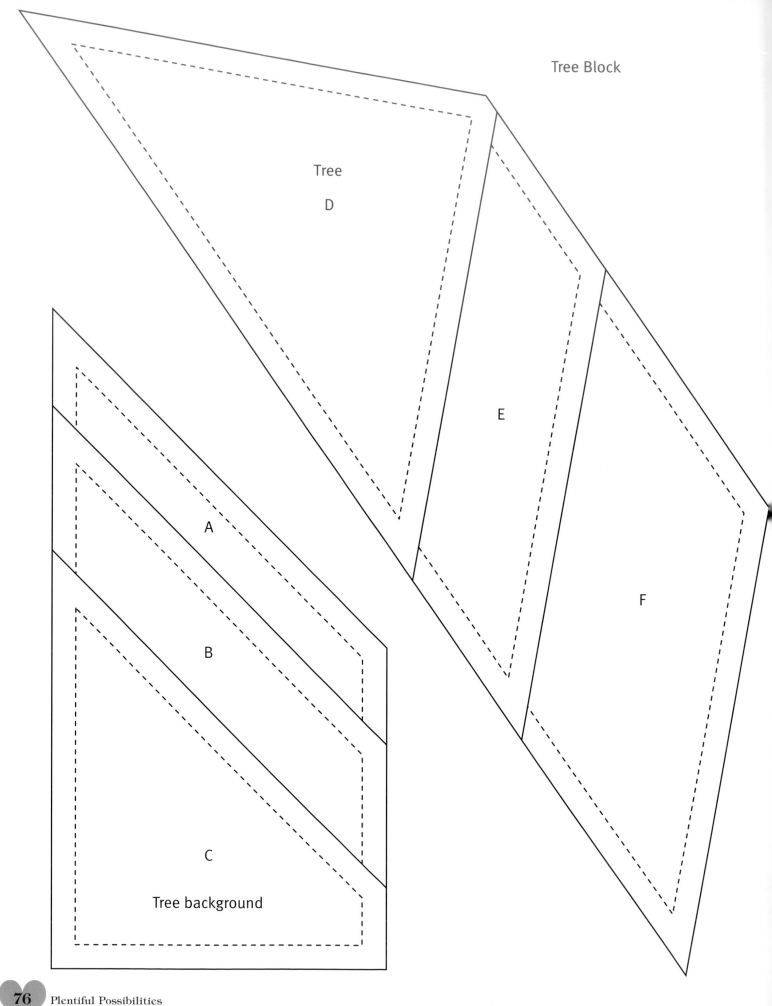

Tree Block

Tree

D

E

F

A

B

C

Tree background

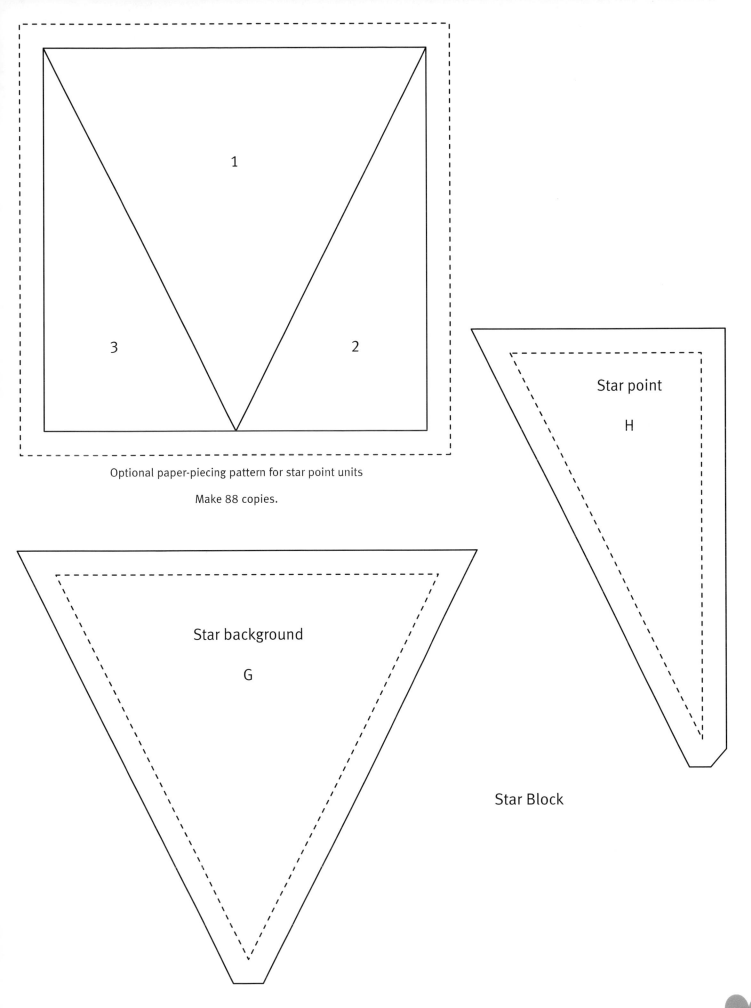

1

3 2

Optional paper-piecing pattern for star point units

Make 88 copies.

Star point

H

Star background

G

Star Block

Enlarge patterns 120% for pillows and 140% for wallhangings.
Patterns are not reversed so lettering can be traced. Reverse the appliqué patterns if you are using fusible web.

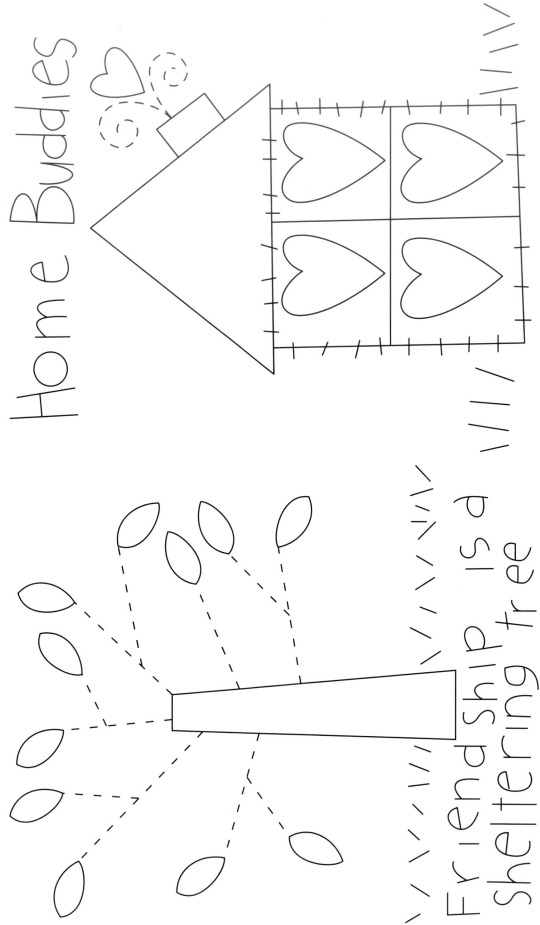

Home Buddies

Friendship is a sheltering tree

Enlarge patterns 120% for pillows and 140% for wallhangings.
Patterns are not reversed so lettering can be traced. Reverse the appliqué patterns if you are using fusible web.

what is a friend?

a single soul dwelling in 2 bodies

aristotle

from the bottom of

My Heart

P·O·C·K·E·T P·A·L·S

Finished block size: 8" x 8"

MATERIALS AND YARDAGE

	Cradle	Crib	Twin
Finished quilt size	36" x 36"	36" x 52"	68" x 100"
Block sets	3 x 3	3 x 5	7 x 11
Total number of blocks	9 (5 pieced)	15 (8 pieced)	77 (39 pieced)
Light print (background and borders)	1³/₄ yards	2 yards	6¹/₄ yards
Blue prints (stars, pockets, and border triangles)	5 prints	8 prints	8 prints**
	¹/₄ yard each	¹/₄ yard each	¹/₂ yard each
Brown check (bears)	³/₈ yard	⁵/₈ yard	**
Red ribbon	2¹/₂ yards	4 yards	¹/₂ yard each bear**
Backing	1¹/₄ yards	1³/₄ yards	6¹/₈ yards
Binding	³/₈ yard	¹/₂ yard	³/₄ yard
Batting	42" x 42"	42" x 58"	74" x 106"

Stuffing, black and red permanent markers, red colored pencil, and template material

CUTTING

	Pattern/Cut Size	Cradle	Crib	Twin
Light print fabric				
Cut 2 lengthwise for Border 1 sides		2¹/₂" x 24¹/₂"	2¹/₂" x 40¹/₂"	2¹/₂" x 88¹/₂"
Cut 2 lengthwise for Border 1 top/bottom		2¹/₂" x 28¹/₂"	2¹/₂" x 28¹/₂"	2¹/₂" x 60¹/₂"
Cut 2 lengthwise for Border 3 sides		2¹/₂" x 32¹/₂"	2¹/₂" x 48¹/₂"	2¹/₂" x 96¹/₂"
Cut 2 lengthwise for Border 3 top/bottom		2¹/₂" x 36¹/₂"	2¹/₂" x 36¹/₂"	2¹/₂" x 68¹/₂"
Setting squares	8¹/₂" x 8¹/₂"	4	7	38
Corner squares for blocks	2¹/₂" x 2¹/₂"	24	36	160
Triangles	2⁷/₈" x 2⁷/₈"*	48	68	232
Blue print fabrics				
Star block center	4¹/₂" x 4¹/₂"	1 each of 5	1 each of 8	5 each of 8
Triangles	2⁷/₈" x 2⁷/₈"*	10 each of 5	9 each of 8	29 each of 8
Pocket	A (page 85)	2 each of 5	2 each of 8	**
Brown check fabric	7" x 7"	10	16	**
Binding fabric				
Cut 2¹/₂" x width of the fabric		4 strips	5 strips	9 strips

* Cut squares in half diagonally for half-square triangles.

** We suggest you make only a few bears and pockets for the twin size quilt. An extra ¹/₄ yard of one of the blue fabrics will make 4 pockets and ³/₈ yard of the brown check will make several bears. An alternative would be to make blocks into 1 or 2 Pocket Pals pillows.

Note: The pieced border in this quilt requires exact piecing of all the elements, so exact lengths for all pieces of the quilt are given.

DIRECTIONS

Refer to Quilting Basics (pages 102–110) as needed for quilt construction techniques. Use a ¼" seam allowance unless otherwise noted.

Block Assembly

Make the number of blocks you need for your selected quilt size.

1. Place 2 pocket pieces (A) right sides together. Stitch along the curved edge. Clip the curve, turn right side out, and press.

2. Place the pocket on a 4½" square with the side edges matching. Make an inverted pleat in the middle along the bottom edge so that all the raw edges match. Press and baste.

Make inverted pleat.

3. Stitch the blue and background triangles into half-square triangle units.

Stitch triangles together.

4. Stitch the blocks as shown. Make the number of blocks you need for your selected quilt size.

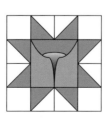

Stitch block together.   Block with pocket

Quilt Assembly

Refer to the Quilt Assembly Diagram.

1. Stitch the blocks and the setting squares into rows. Be sure the pockets open toward the top of the quilt. Press the seam allowances in alternate directions for each row, so the seams nest when the rows are stitched together.

2. Stitch the rows together. Press.

Border 1
1. Stitch the Border 1 side strips to the sides of the quilt. Press. Stitch the remaining Border 1 strips to the top and bottom of the quilt. Press.

Border 2
1. Piece the blue and background triangles into squares and stitch the squares together to make the length you need for your selected quilt size.
• For the cradle size, make 56 half-square triangle units. Make 4 borders of 14 units each.
• For the crib size, make 72 half-square triangle units. Make 2 borders of 14 units each and 2 borders of 22 units each.
• For the twin size, make 152 half-square triangle units. Make 2 borders of 30 units each and 2 borders of 46 units each.

When piecing, be sure to alternate the direction of the triangles at the midpoint of each side.

Change direction of triangles at center.
2. Stitch the side borders to the quilt top. Press. Then stitch the top and bottom borders to the quilt top. Press.

Border 3
1. Stitch the Border 3 side strips to the sides of the quilt. Press. Stitch the remaining Border 3 strips to the top and bottom of the quilt. Press.

Finishing

1. Piece the backing so it is the same size as the batting. Layer and quilt as desired. Trim the backing and batting even with the quilt top.

2. Bind the quilt using a ³⁄₈" seam allowance. Refer to pages 109–110 for information on bindings.

Quilt Assembly Diagram

TEDDY BEARS

1. Use pattern B to make a template for the bears.

2. Place 2 squares of the bear fabric right sides together. Place the template on the wrong side of the top fabric and trace around the template. Do not cut yet.

3. Stitch on the drawn line, leaving the seam open between the x's.

4. Cut out, adding a scant ¹⁄₄" seam allowance. Clip the curves and inside points. Turn right side out.

5. Tack the base of each ear together with a few small stitches. Stuff the teddy, leaving the ears unstuffed. Stitch the opening closed.

6. Use a black marker to make eyes. Use a red marker for the nose and mouth. Blush the cheeks with a red pencil.

7. Give each bear a ribbon bow tie.

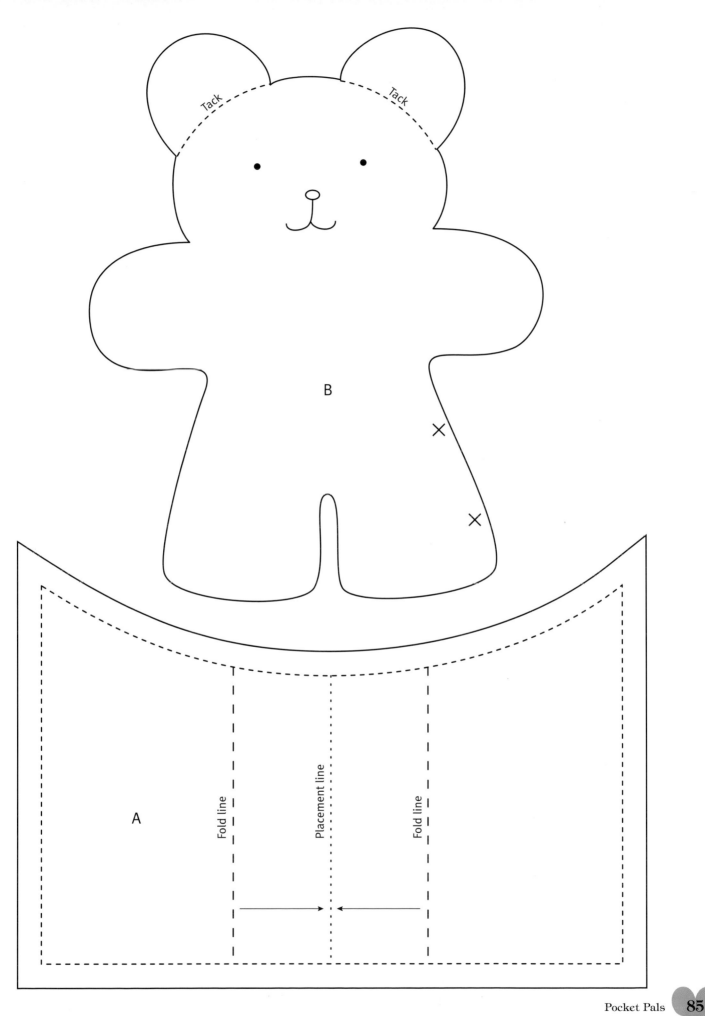

Tack

Tack

B

A

Fold line

Placement line

Fold line

Finished block size: 24" x 24"
Finished quilt size: 48" x 48"

MATERIALS AND YARDAGE

Yellow 2 yards for background
Green print 1 yard for leaf/stems and triangles
Pink print ⅝ yard for tulips and triangles
Floral print 1 yard for trapezoids and triangles
Backing 3¼ yards
Binding ½ yard
Batting 54" x 54"
Fusible web (optional for fusible appliqué)

CUTTING

Patterns are on page 90.

This quilt can be made using the Easy Triangles technique for the half-square triangle units. For the Easy Triangle method, you will need 2 copies of page 101. Alternate cutting directions are given if you prefer not to use Easy Triangles.

Yellow fabric
Center square: Cut 4 squares 6½" x 6½".
Triangles: Cut 16 squares 3⅞" x 3⅞", then cut each in half diagonally.
Corner triangles: Cut 8 squares 12⅞" x 12⅞", then cut each in half diagonally.

Green print fabric
Leaf/stem appliqués: Cut 16 using pattern A.
Triangles: Cut 16 squares 5⅛" x 5⅛", then cut each in half diagonally.

Pink print fabric
Tulip appliqués: Cut 16 using pattern A.
Half-square triangles: Cut either 2 squares 8½" x 8½" for Easy Triangles *or* cut 8 squares 3⅞" x 3⅞", then cut each in half diagonally

Floral print fabric
Trapezoids: Cut 32 using pattern B.
Half-square triangles: Cut either 2 squares 8½" x 8½" for Easy Triangles *or* cut 8 squares 3⅞" x 3⅞", then cut each in half diagonally.

Binding fabric
Cut 5 strips 2¼" x width of the fabric.

DIRECTIONS

Refer to Quilting Basics (pages 102–110) as needed for quilt construction techniques. Use a ¼" seam allowance unless otherwise noted.

Block Assembly

1. Make 16 half-square triangle units for the blocks, using the pink print and floral print fabrics. Use the 3" finished Easy Triangles (refer to page 101), or piece together triangles cut from the 3⅞" squares.

Make 16.

2. Make 16 Flying Geese units for the blocks, using the yellow fabric and green print fabric.

Make 16.

3. The corner triangle unit is made with two trapezoids and a triangle, and has a set-in point. When piecing, stitch only to the seam intersection (¼" from the edge), not to the cut edges. Press.

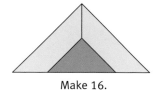

Make 16.

4. Piece the blocks as shown. Make 4 blocks.

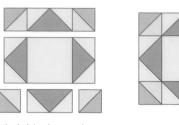

Stitch block together.   Make 4.

5. Stitch the corner triangle units from Step 3 to the blocks made in Step 4 .

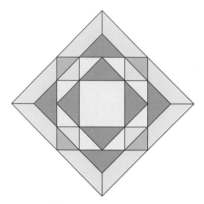

Add corner triangle units.

6. Stitch 1 yellow corner triangle to each side of each block. Press.

Add corner triangles.

7. Appliqué the tulips and leaf/stems on the corners of each block.

Quilt Assembly

Refer to the Quilt Assembly Diagram.

1. Stitch the blocks into rows. Press.

2. Stitch the rows together. Press.

Finishing

1. Piece the backing so it is the same size as the batting. Layer and quilt as desired. Trim the backing and batting even with the quilt top.

2. Bind the quilt using a $1/4$" seam allowance. Refer to pages 109–110 for information on bindings.

Quilt Assembly Diagram

PRAIRIE TULIPS PILLOW

Finished size: 24" x 24"

MATERIALS AND YARDAGE

Yellow 2 1/8 yards for background and pillow back
Green print 1/4 yard for leaf/stems and triangles
Pink print 1/4 yard for tulips and triangles
Floral print 1/4 yard for trapezoids and triangles
Backing for quilting 7/8 yard
Binding 1/4 yard
Batting 26" x 26"
Pillow form 24" x 24"
Fusible web (optional for fusible appliqué)

CUTTING

Patterns are on page 90.

Yellow fabric
Center square: Cut 1 square 6 1/2" x 6 1/2".
Triangles: Cut 4 squares 3 7/8" x 3 7/8", then cut each in half diagonally.
Corner triangles: Cut 2 squares 12 7/8" x 12 7/8", then cut each in half diagonally.
Pillow back: Cut 2 rectangles 24 1/2" x 36".

Green print fabric
Leaf/stem appliqués: Cut 4 using pattern A.
Triangles: Cut 4 squares 5 1/8" x 5 1/8", then cut each in half diagonally.

Pink print fabric
Tulip appliqués: Cut 4 using pattern A.
Half-square triangles: Cut 2 squares 3 7/8" x 3 7/8", then cut each in half diagonally.

Floral print fabric
Trapezoids: Cut 8 using pattern B.
Half-square triangles: Cut 2 squares 3 7/8" x 3 7/8", then cut each in half diagonally.

Backing for quilting
Cut 1 square 26" x 26".

Binding fabric
Cut 3 strips 2 1/4" x width of the fabric.

DIRECTIONS

Use a 1/4" seam allowance unless otherwise noted.

1. Piece and appliqué the block as described in Block Assembly on pages 87–88.

2. Layer the block with batting and backing fabric. Quilt as desired.

3. Trim the backing and the batting even with the pillow top.

4. Make the envelope back by pressing each pillow back piece in half, wrong sides together. When folded, each will measure 18" x 24 1/2". Place both pieces on the wrong side of the pillow top, matching raw edges and overlapping the folded edges in the center. Baste the raw edges together.

5. Bind the pillow using a 1/4" seam allowance. Refer to pages 109–110 for information on bindings.

Pillow Assembly Diagram

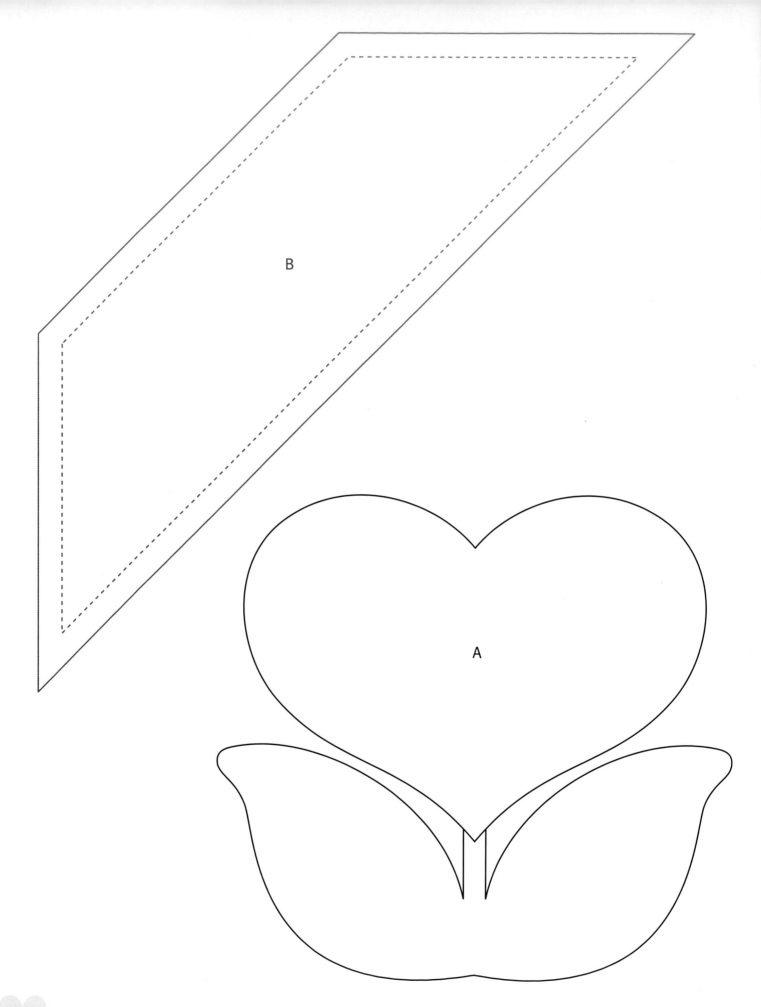

B

A

P·S· I L·O·V·E Y·O·U

Finished block size: 3" x 3"

MATERIALS AND YARDAGE

	Cradle	Crib	Twin
Finished quilt size	31" x 37"	45" x 57"	63" x 99"
Block sets	7 x 9	11 x 13	17 x 25
Total number of blocks	63	143	425
	32 Nine-Patch	72 Nine-Patch	213 Nine-Patch
	31 alternate	71 alternate	212 alternate
White background and border	1 ¼ yards	3 yards	5 ¾ yards
Colored scraps to total	¾ yard	1 ¼ yards	2 ½ yards
Backing	1 ⅛ yards	3 yards	6 yards
Binding	⅜ yard	½ yard	¾ yard
Batting	37" x 43"	51" x 63"	69" x 105"

Fusible web (optional for fusible appliqué)

CUTTING

	Pattern / Cut Size	Cradle	Crib	Twin
White fabric				
Cut 4 for sides, top, and bottom	5 ½" x width of the fabric			
Cut 2 lengthwise for the sides			*6 ½" x 57 ½"	*6 ½" x 99 ½"
Cut 1 lengthwise for the top			*12 ½" x 33 ½"	*18 ½" x 51 ½"
Cut 1 lengthwise for the bottom			*6 ½" x 33 ½"	*6 ½" x 51 ½"
Alternate blocks	3 ½" x 3 ½"	31	71	212
Nine-Patch blocks	1 ½" x 1 ½"	128	288	852
Scraps for Nine-Patch blocks	1 ½" x 1 ½"	160	360	1065
Girl/boy & letters**	Pages 95–98		1 set	1 set
Hearts**	Page 98	**	6 large	**
			74 others	
Binding fabric				
2 ½" x width of the fabric		4 strips	6 strips	9 strips

* Cut these borders on the lengthwise grain, then cut the squares for the blocks from the remaining fabric. Border lengths may need to be adjusted to your quilt.

** For the cradle size quilt, use only hearts. For the twin quilt, cut any number of hearts of any size, depending on how far down the sides of the quilt you want them.

Note: Letters are included for IT'S A BOY, IT'S A GIRL, and PS I LOVE YOU.

DIRECTIONS

Refer to Quilting Basics (pages 102–110) as needed for quilt construction techniques. Use a ¼" seam allowance unless otherwise noted.

Block Assembly

Make the number of blocks you need for your selected quilt size.

1. Refer to the Materials and Yardage chart for the total number of blocks. Use 5 colored and 4 white 1½" x 1½" squares for each Nine-Patch block.

2. Make the Nine-Patch blocks as shown. Press.

Stitch block together.

Nine-Patch block

Quilt Assembly

Refer to the Quilt Assembly Diagram.

1. Arrange the blocks in rows. Be sure the odd rows begin with Nine-Patch blocks and the even rows begin with background blocks.

2. Stitch the blocks into rows. Press the seams in alternate directions, so they nest when the rows are stitched together.

3. Stitch the rows together. Press.

Border

1. Measure the width of the quilt. Adjust the top and bottom border strips to the measured length, and stitch to the top and bottom of the quilt. Press. Measure the length of the quilt (including the top and bottom borders). Adjust the side border strips to the measured length, and stitch to the sides of the quilt. Press.

2. Appliqué the desired lettering and hearts onto the border. On the twin quilt, place the girl or boy near the bottom edge of the top border, close to the block section of the quilt, so it will be centered on the pillow when the bed is made.

Finishing

1. Piece the backing so it is the same size as the batting. Layer and quilt as desired. Trim the backing and batting even with the quilt top.

2. Bind the quilt using a ⅜" seam allowance. Refer to pages 109–110 for information on bindings.

Quilt Assembly Diagram

P.S. I LOVE YOU PILLOW

Finished pillow size: 13¹/₂" x 13¹/₂"

MATERIALS AND YARDAGE

Background ¹/₂ yard
A variety of scraps for the appliqués—refer to
  patterns on pages 95–98 for size
Pillow back ¹/₂ yard
Binding ¹/₄ yard
Pillow form 14" x 14"

CUTTING

Background fabric

Cut 1 square 14" x 14".

Pillow back fabric

Cut 2 rectangles 14" x 20".

Binding fabric

Cut 3 strips 2¹/₄" x width of the fabric.

DIRECTIONS

Use a ¹/₄" seam allowance unless otherwise noted.

1. Appliqué the girl or boy and the desired hearts on the pillow background.

2. Make the envelope back by pressing each pillow back piece in half, wrong sides together. When folded, each will measure 14" x 10". Place both pieces on the wrong side of the pillow top, matching raw edges and overlapping the folded edges in the center. Baste the raw edges together.

3. Bind the pillow using a ¹/₄" seam allowance. Refer to pages 109–110 for information on bindings.

4. Insert the pillow form.

QUILT LABEL

Refer to page 19 for instructions on making quilt labels.

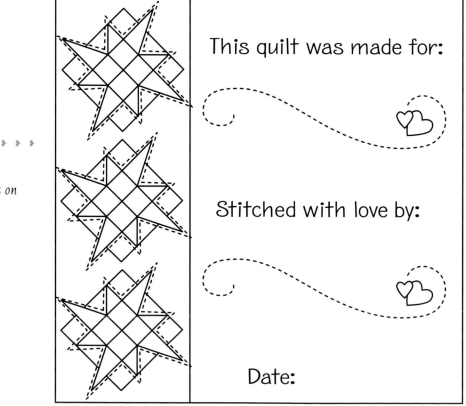

This quilt was made for:

Stitched with love by:

Date:

Patterns are reversed for tracing to fusible web.

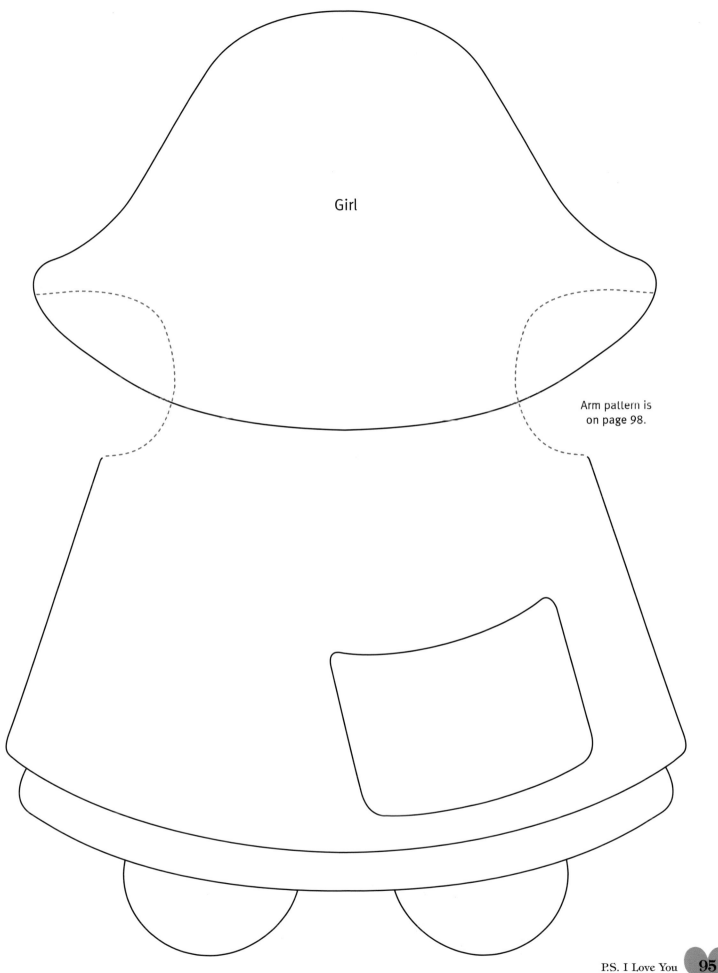

Girl

Arm pattern is
on page 98.

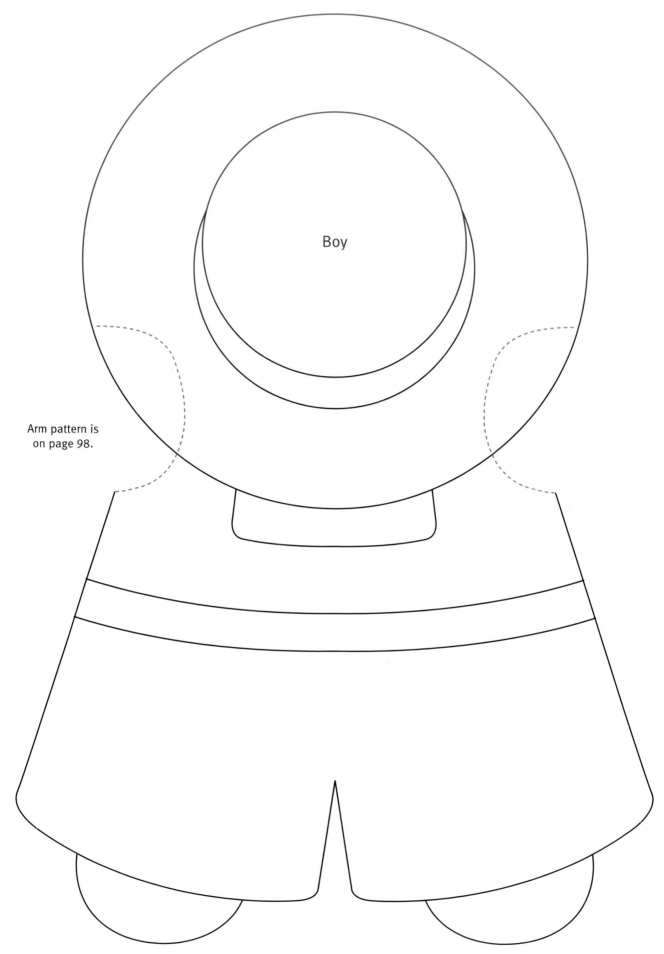

Boy

Arm pattern is
on page 98.

Patterns are reversed for tracing to fusible web.

Girl's Arm

Cut 1.
Cut 1 reversed.

Boy's Arm

Cut 1.
Cut 1 reversed.

1. Make the required number of copies on a photocopier that reproduces at an accurate 100%. Check the first copy for accuracy before making the rest of the copies. Use a lightweight paper that tears away easily. Test the paper before making copies to make sure that it is easy to tear away. Each page will yield 8 half-square triangle units.

2. Place the selected fabrics right sides together. Make as many sets as needed.

3. Place an Easy Triangle copy on top of the fabric. Center carefully and pin.

4. Stitch on all the *dashed* lines. Use a slightly smaller than usual stitch (15 stitches per inch or 1.5 to 1.8 on some machines).

5. Cut on all *solid* lines, including the outside lines, with a rotary cutter and ruler.

6. Carefully tear away the paper.

7. Gently press the half-square triangle units open.

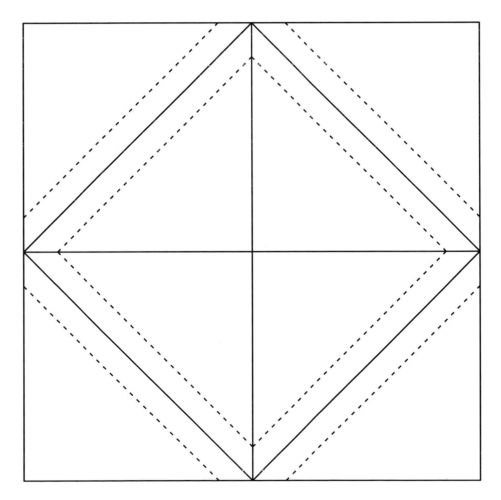

$1^{1}/_{2}$" Finished Easy Triangles

Stitch on dashed lines and cut on solid lines.
Use a short stitch length (15 stitches per inch or 1.5–1.8 on some machines) to make it easier to tear away the paper.

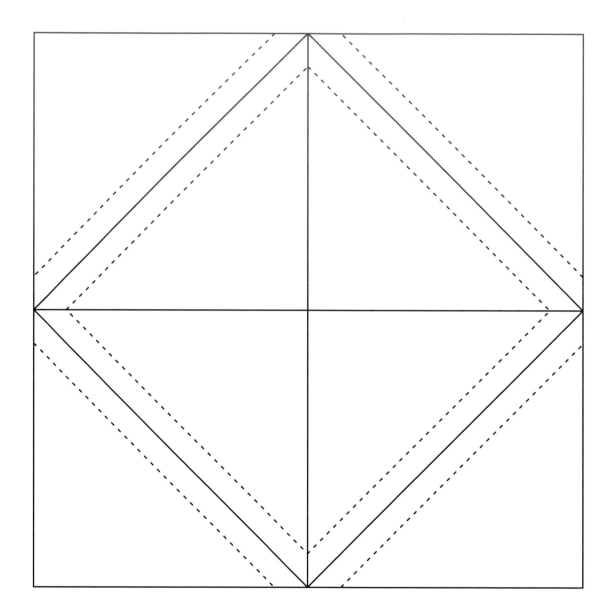

2" Finished Easy Triangles

Stitch on dashed lines and cut on solid lines.

Use a short stitch length (15 stitches per inch or 1.5–1.8 on some machines) to make it easier to tear away the paper.

Refer to page 99 for complete instructions.

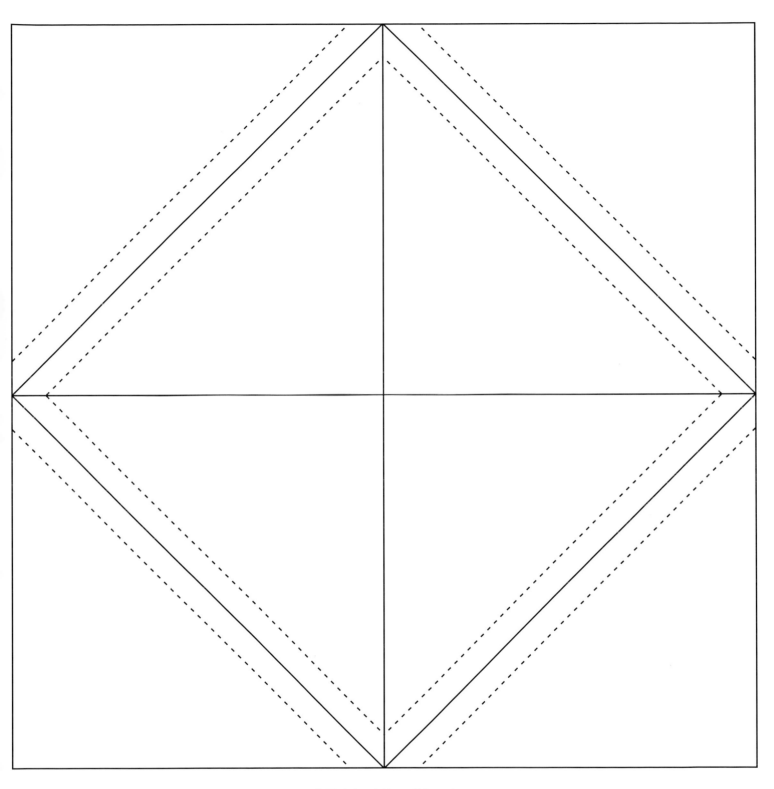

3" Finished Easy Triangles

Stitch on dashed lines and cut on solid lines.

Use a short stitch length (15 stitches per inch or 1.5–1.8 on some machines) to make it easier to tear away the paper.

Refer to page 99 for complete instructions.

FABRIC

We recommend using 100% cotton fabric for making quilts. Fabric requirements are based on a 42" width, but many fabrics shrink when washed, and widths vary by manufacturer, so yardage is calculated based on 40". Prewash fabric and check for colorfastness before using.

SEAM ALLOWANCES

A ¼" seam allowance is used for most projects. It is a good idea to do a test seam before you begin stitching to check that your ¼" is accurate.

ROTARY CUTTING

For squares and rectangles, follow the cutting instructions for each project.

Odd-sized and asymmetrical pieces can be cut quickly with a rotary cutter. Cut around the paper pattern, making sure the pattern includes the ¼" seam allowance. Layer the fabric either by folding (which will result in original-image and reverse-image pieces) or by stacking fabric pieces with the right side up (which will result only in original-image pieces). Tape the pattern to the top layer of the fabric with a loop of tape. Use a rotary cutter and small ruler to cut around the pattern, moving the ruler as needed.

PIECING

1. Be sure to use a ¼" seam allowance when stitching.

2. Use a light neutral thread when stitching most fabrics. If all the fabrics are dark, use a dark thread.

3. Place the pieces to be joined right sides together. Pin, matching raw edges and any seamlines, and sew with a straight stitch (10–12 stitches per inch, depending on your machine). Press the seam allowances toward the darker fabric, unless otherwise noted.

4. To save time and thread, chain piece by stitching a seam and then immediately feeding in a new set of pieces without lifting the presser foot or clipping the threads. Stitch as many sets as needed, then clip them apart.

5. Where two seams meet, position one seam allowance in one direction and the other seam allowance in the opposite direction. Push the seams together tightly; they will hold each other in place as you stitch. This is often called "nesting" the seams. It is usually not necessary to pin.

Nest the seams.

6. When stitching across triangular intersection seams (as with Flying Geese), aim for the point where the seamlines intersect. This will avoid cutting off the points.

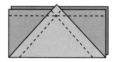

Stitch across at the point.

7. When squares are cut in half on the diagonal, the cut units are called half-square triangles. When half-square triangles are stitched together, the square they form is called a half-square triangle unit because it is made from two half-square triangles. Many of the projects in this book use half-square triangle units. You can make half-square triangle units either by using the Easy Triangle method described on page 99, or by cutting the given squares on the diagonal and piecing the appropriate pairs together.

Cut on diagonal.   Stitch together.   Finished unit

8. When piecing, if one of the edges to be pieced appears to be larger, put that side down (next to the feed dogs) so the extra fabric will be eased into the seam without leaving tucks.

MACHINE APPLIQUÉ USING FUSIBLE WEB

1. Trace the patterns onto the smooth, paper side of the fusible web. Unless otherwise noted, the patterns in this book have already been reversed and are ready to be traced.

2. Use paper-cutting scissors to roughly cut out the traced pieces, adding at least $^1/_4$" around the edges of each pattern.

3. Follow the manufacturer's instructions to iron the fusible web pieces to the wrong side of the selected appliqué fabric. Use a non-stick appliqué-pressing sheet to avoid getting adhesive on your iron or ironing board.

4. Cut out the fused pieces along the traced line. Do not remove the paper until you are ready to fuse the pieces to your project.

5. When you are ready to appliqué, remove the paper and position the appliqué piece on your project. Be sure the web (rough) side is down. Press in place, following the manufacturer's instructions. If the design is layered, arrange all the appliqué pieces before fusing.

6. The raw edges of the appliqué pieces can be finished with a satin stitch, buttonhole stitch, or invisible zigzag stitch.

HAND APPLIQUÉ

Unless otherwise noted, the patterns in this book have already been reversed for fusible appliqué. You will need to reverse the images if you are doing hand appliqué.

1. Make plastic templates from the patterns. Do not include seam or turn-under allowances when making the templates.

2. For each appliqué piece you need, place the template on the right side of the selected fabric. Draw around the template, keeping the template at least $^1/_4$" away from the selvages.

3. Cut out the appliqué pieces, adding a $^3/_{16}$" turn-under allowance.

4. Turn under and baste all edges that will not be overlapped by another piece. Fold the edges under on the drawn line and baste in place with a single thread. Clip the seam allowance on the inside curves and points, allowing the fabric to spread.

Clip at inside curves.

Clip the inside angles up to the seamline. When appliquéing these angles, take small overcast stitches to prevent fraying.

Clip inside angle.   Fold.

Miter the outside points when the angle is less than 90°. Trim off the point, then miter using 3 separate folds.

1. Fold down the point.
2. Fold one edge to the seamline.
3. Fold the other edge to the seamline. It may be necessary to trim the corner before folding to reduce bulk.

Miter outside points.

5. Pin or baste the pieces to the background fabric.

6. Appliqué, using thread that matches the appliqué piece. Knot the thread and hide the knot under the appliqué. Stitch from right to left, bringing the needle out through the folded edge of the appliqué. Insert the needle into the background directly across from where the thread emerges from the fold and bring it up approximately $1/8$" away, catching only 1 or 2 threads of the folded edge of the appliqué. Stitch all the way around the appliqué piece.

7. End by bringing the needle to the back and knotting off.

PAPER PIECING

Paper piecing can be used to create very accurate blocks. For *Cinnamon Hearts* and *Path Through the Pines*, an optional pattern is provided to paper piece a block made of three triangles.

Note: You stitch on the side of the paper with the printed lines and place the fabric on the non-printed side.

1. Trace or photocopy the number of paper-piecing patterns needed.

2. Use a smaller-than-usual stitch length (1.5–1.8 or 18–20 stitches per inch, depending on your machine), and a slightly larger needle (size 90/14). This makes the paper removal easier, and will result in tighter stitches that will not be pulled apart when you tear the paper off.

3. Cut the pieces slightly larger than necessary—about $3/4$" larger; they do not need to be perfect shapes. (One of the joys of paper piecing!)

4. Pin the first piece of fabric to the center of the block on the non-printed side of the paper, but make sure you do not place the pin anywhere near a seamline. Hold the paper up to the light to make sure the piece covers the area it is supposed to, with the seam allowance also amply covered.

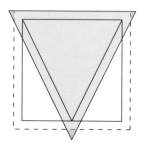

Place fabric on non-printed side of paper.

5. Fold the pattern back at the stitching lines and trim the fabric to a $1/4$" seam allowance with a ruler and rotary cutter.

6. Cut the side triangles large enough to cover the side areas plus a generous seam allowance. It is a good idea to cut each piece larger than you think necessary; it might be a bit wasteful, but is easier than ripping out tiny stitches! Align the edge of the side triangle with the trimmed seam allowance of the center, right sides together, and pin. With the paper side up, stitch on the line.

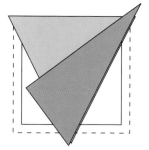

Align next piece with trimmed edge.

7. Open the side piece and press.

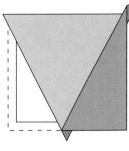

Open and press.

8. Stitch the other side triangle and press open.

9. Trim all around the finished unit on the dashed line, leaving a ¹⁄₄" seam allowance. Leave the paper intact until after the blocks have been stitched together, then carefully remove the paper.

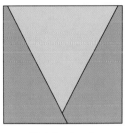

Finished unit

PRESSING

Seam allowances are usually pressed to one side or the other, and it is preferable that they be pressed toward the darker fabric. If this is not possible, make sure that dark fabric seams do not show through a lighter fabric by trimming a scant amount from the dark seam allowance.

Press lightly with an up-and-down motion, using steam. Avoid using a very hot iron or over-ironing, which can distort shapes and blocks.

When two seams meet, stitch and press one seam allowance in one direction and the other seam allowance in the other direction. This will allow the seams to nest and fit tightly together.

When pressing sashing, press the seam allowance toward the sashing strips. When pressing borders, press the seam allowance toward the outside edges.

BORDERS

When border strips are cut crosswise, diagonally piece the strips together to achieve the needed length.

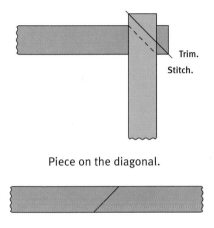

Piece on the diagonal.

Press open.

Butted Borders

1. In most cases the side borders are stitched on first. When you have finished the quilt top, measure the length of the quilt top from cut edge to cut edge in several places. Do not measure along the edge of the quilt as it is often stretched and will measure longer than a measurement taken through the center. Take an average of the measurements. This will be the length to cut the side borders.

Measure.

2. Fold one side border and one side of the quilt top into quarters and mark the folds with pins. Match the marked points and pin the border to the quilt, right sides together. This distributes any ease along the entire edge of the quilt. Mark and pin the other side border.

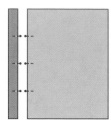

Pin the marked points.

3. Stitch the borders to the quilt, using a $1/4$" seam allowance.

4. Press the seam allowances toward the outside edge of the quilt.

5. Repeat the process for the top and bottom borders.

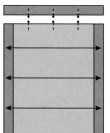

Repeat for top and bottom borders.

Mitered Corner Borders

1. Measure the length of the quilt top from seamline to seamline in several places. Do not measure along the edge of the quilt as it is often stretched and will measure longer than a measurement taken through the center. Take an average of the measurements and add 2 times the width of your border, plus 2" to 4" extra. This is the length you need to cut for the side borders.

2. Find the center of the long inside edge of one side border and mark it with a pin. Measure from the pin in each direction, one-half the quilt length measurement, and mark with pins. These marks correspond to the corner seam intersections on the quilt top. Mark the other side border.

3. Find the center of the quilt side by folding the quilt in half, and mark the center with a pin. Pin the side border to the quilt, right sides together, matching the center and seam intersections. Mark and pin the other side border.

4. Stitch the side borders to the quilt, stopping and backstitching at the seam intersection, $1/4$" in from the edge. The excess length will extend beyond each edge. Press the seams toward the outer edge of the quilt.

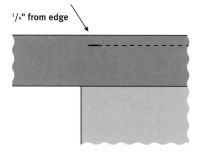

$1/4$" from edge

Stop stitching $1/4$" from edge.

5. Repeat the process for the top and bottom borders.

6. To create the miter, lay a corner on the ironing board. Working with the quilt right side up, lay one border strip on top of the adjacent border. You may want to pin the quilt to the ironing board to keep it from slipping.

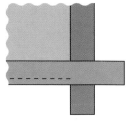

Overlap borders at corner.

7. With the borders overlapping, fold one border under at a 45° angle. Match the seams or stripes and work with it until it matches perfectly.

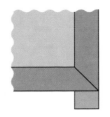

Fold under at a 45° angle.

8. Position a 90° triangle or ruler over the corner to check that the corner is flat and square. When everything is in place, press the fold firmly.

Square corner.

9. Fold the center section of the quilt top diagonally from the corner, right sides together, and align the long edges of the border strips. On the wrong side, place pins near the pressed fold in the corner to secure the border strips.

10. Beginning at the inside corner, backstitch, and then stitch along the fold toward the outside point, being careful not to allow any stretching to occur. Backstitch at the end. Trim the excess border fabric to a ¼" seam allowance. Press the seam open.

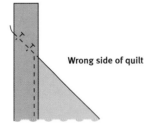

Wrong side of quilt

Stitch toward the outside edge.

MARKING FOR QUILTING

Plan a density of quilting that corresponds to the requirements of the chosen batting; some batting requires stitching to be closer together than other batting.

There are many marking tools available, including a variety of pencils, chalk, soapstone, and air- or water-soluble markers. Be sure to test your chosen marking tool on a sample of your quilt fabric to make sure that the marks can be completely removed when you are finished quilting. Masking tape works well to mark straight lines.

BACKING

Plan on making the backing a minimum of 2" to 3" larger than the quilt top on all sides. **For larger quilts that require pieced backings, piece the backing either horizontally or vertically; or to economize, you can piece the backing from leftover fabrics or blocks.** Prewash the backing fabric, and trim the selvages before use.

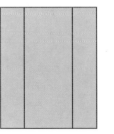
Twin

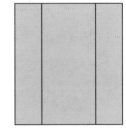
Full or Double

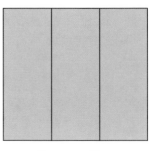
Queen or King

Suggested Vertical Piecing

BATTING

The type of batting to use is a personal decision; consult your local quilt shop. Cut batting at least 2" larger than your quilt top on all sides. Be sure to coordinate the density of the quilting with the batting and the design of the quilt top.

LAYERING

To layer the backing, batting, and quilt top, spread the backing wrong side up and tape the edges down with masking tape. If you are working on carpet, you can use T-pins to secure the backing to the carpet. Center the batting on top, smoothing out any folds. Place the quilt top right side up on top of the batting and backing, making sure it is centered. Trim the batting to the same size as the backing, if the batting is bigger.

BASTING

Basting joins the three layers (quilt top, batting, and backing) together in preparation for quilting.

If you plan to machine quilt, pin baste the quilt layers together with 1" brass safety pins placed a minimum of 4" to 6" apart. Begin basting in the center and move toward the edges, placing the pins where they will not be in the way of the planned quilting.

An alternative to pin basting is spray baste, sold in aerosol cans.

If you plan to hand quilt, baste the layers together with thread using a long needle and light-colored thread. Knot one end of the thread. Use stitches approximately the length of the needle, and begin in the center and move out toward the edges. A sunburst design or grid pattern works well. After the quilt is basted, roll the outside edges of the backing and batting to the front of the quilt and baste in place.

This will protect the edges of the batting during quilting. As quilting stitches are added, the basting stitches can be removed.

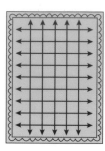
Grid pattern

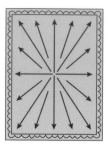
Sunburst pattern

QUILTING

Quilting, whether by hand or machine, enhances the pieced or appliqué design of the quilt. You may choose to quilt in-the-ditch, echo the pieced or appliqué motifs, use patterns from quilting design books and stencils, or do your own free-motion quilting. As mentioned previously, be sure to coordinate the density of the quilting with the batting and the design of the quilt top.

TYING A QUILT

Tying a quilt is an alternative to hand or machine quilting. You can use pearl cotton, six-strand embroidery floss, or fine crochet cotton.

1. After you baste the quilt, use a darning needle to tie the quilt at the intervals required by the chosen batting. Work from the center out. Insert the needle through all layers and come up approximately 1/8" away. Take an identical stitch directly on top of the first one. Move to the next spot without cutting the thread.

2. Repeat Step 1 until the thread runs out. Rethread the needle and continue until the whole quilt is secured with stitches.

3. Clip the thread in the middle between the stitches. Tie a square knot at each point. Trim the thread ends, leaving at least 1/2".

BINDING

A double-fold binding is recommended because of its durability. Bias binding is not needed unless you are binding curved edges.

Trim the excess batting and backing from the quilt. For a ³/₈" finished binding cut the binding strips 2¹/₂" wide. For a ¹/₄" finished binding (used on quilts with star points at the edge), cut the binding strips 2¹/₄" wide. Piece the strips together as needed with a diagonal seam to make a continuous binding strip. (See page 105 for instructions on making a diagonal seam.) The diagonal seam will reduce bulk when you stitch the binding to the quilt. Press the seams open, then press the entire strip in half lengthwise with wrong sides together.

Stairstep Corners

1. Attach the binding strips in the same order as you attached the borders. Pin the binding to one edge of the front side of the quilt, raw edges even. Stitch using a ¹/₄" or ³/₈" seam allowance as directed. If possible, use an even-feed or walking foot to prevent the binding from "scooting" ahead. Repeat on the opposite side of the quilt front.

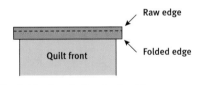

Attach binding to front of quilt.

2. Bring the binding over the raw edge so that the fold of the binding comes to the stitched line on the back. Pin the binding in place on the back at the four corners.

Pin binding on back.

3. Pin the binding to the other two sides of the quilt front. Allow the binding to extend ¹/₂" at the ends. Stitch using a ³/₈" seam allowance. Fold the extended portion of the binding in before bringing the binding to the back.

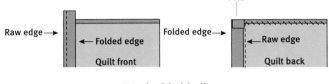

Attach side bindings.

4. Hand stitch the binding to the back of the quilt.

Mitered Corners

1. With raw edges even, pin the binding to the edge of the quilt at least 12" away from a corner. Leave the first 6" of the binding unattached. Start stitching, using a ¹/₄" or ³/₈" seam allowance as directed.

2. Stop ¹/₄" or ³/₈" away from the first corner. Leave the needle in the fabric and pivot the quilt 90°. Backstitch to the edge.

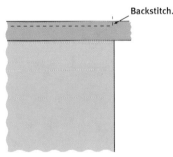

Stop and pivot quilt.

3. Lift the presser foot and needle. Pull the quilt slightly away from the machine, leaving the threads attached. Fold the binding so it extends straight above the quilt.

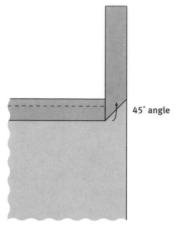

45° angle

Fold binding straight up.

4. Bring the binding strip down even with the edge of the quilt. Resume stitching at the top edge.

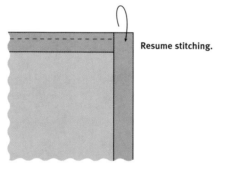

Resume stitching.

Fold binding down.

5. After making all four of the mitered corners, stop stitching 6" from the beginning stitching. Take the quilt out of the sewing machine. Place the ends of the binding along the unstitched edge of the quilt. Trim the ends so they overlap by ¹/₂".

6. Unfold the binding. Place the ends of the binding right sides together and stitch with a ¹/₄" seam. Finger-press the seam open, refold the binding, and stitch the remaining binding to the quilt.

7. Turn the binding to the back of the quilt and hand stitch the folded edge to just cover the stitched line. To distribute bulk, fold each corner miter in the opposite direction from where it was folded and stitched on the front.

ABOUT THE AUTHORS

Nancy and Lynda

In 1981 Nancy Smith and Lynda Milligan joined forces to establish the Great American Quilt Factory, Inc. The store, in Denver, Colorado, specialized in quilting patterns, fabrics, classes, and supplies. Four years later, Nancy and Lynda began designing patterns for quilts, stuffed animals, and dolls. In 1985, they formed DreamSpinners, the pattern division of Great American Quilt Factory, Inc.

In 1987 the business needed more space, and moved to its present location on East Hampden Avenue in Denver. Consequently, DreamSpinners continued to grow, and eventually became the largest independent pattern company in the United States.

In 1988, Nancy and Lynda created Possibilities as a book publishing division. To date, Possibilities has published 54 titles. In 1992, the I'll Teach Myself series was created to introduce sewing to a younger generation.

Today, Lynda and Nancy continue to maintain the retail store. They also design lines of fabric for AvLyn, Inc. and VIP/Cranston Consumer Products.

INDEX

Projects

Useful Information

Other Fine Books from C&T Publishing

15 Two-Block Quilts: Unlock the Secrets of Secondary Patterns, Claudia Olson

24 Quilted Gems: Sparkling Traditional & Original Projects, Gai Perry

250 Continuous-Line Quilting Designs for Hand, Machine & Long-Arm Quilters, Laura Lee Fritz

All About Quilting from A to Z, From the Editors and Contributors of Quilter's Newsletter Magazine and Quiltmaker Magazine

America from the Heart: Quilters Remember September 11, 2001, Karey Bresenhan

Appliqué 12 Easy Ways!: Charming Quilts, Giftable Projects, & Timeless Techniques, Elly Sienkiewicz

Appliqué Inside the Lines: 12 Quilt Projects to Embroider & Appliqué, Carol Armstrong

Art of Classic Quiltmaking, The, Harriet Hargrave & Sharyn Craig

At Piece With Time: A Woman's Journey Stitched in Cloth, Kristin Steiner & Diane Frankenberger

Beautifully Quilted with Alex Anderson: • How to Choose or Create the Best Designs for Your Quilt • 6 Timeless Projects • Full-Size Patterns, Ready to Use, Alex Anderson

Best of Baltimore Beauties, The: 95 Patterns for Album Blocks and Borders, Elly Sienkiewicz

Block Magic: Over 50 Fun & Easy Blocks from Squares and Rectangles, Nancy Johnson-Srebro

Block Magic, Too!: Over 50 NEW Blocks from Squares and Rectangles, Nancy Johnson-Srebro

Butterflies & Blooms: Designs for Appliqué & Quilting, Carol Armstrong

Celebrate the Tradition with C&T Publishing: Over 70 Fabulous New Blocks, Tips & Stories from Quilting's Best, C&T Staff

Color Play: Easy Steps to Imaginative Color in Quilts, Joen Wolfrom

Cotton Candy Quilts: Using Feed Sacks, Vintage, and Reproduction Fabrics, Mary Mashuta

Create Your Own Quilt Labels!, Kim Churbuck

Dresden Flower Garden: A New Twist on Two Quilt Classics, Blanche Young & Lynette Young Bingham

Elm Creek Quilts: Quilt Projects Inspired by the Elm Creek Quilts Novels, Jennifer Chiaverini & Nancy Odom

Enchanted Views: Quilts Inspired by Wrought-Iron Designs, Dilys Fronks

Fabric Shopping with Alex Anderson, Alex Anderson

Fantastic Fabric Folding: Innovative Quilting Projects, Rebecca Wat

Fantastic Fans: Exquisite Quilts & Other Projects, Alice Dunsdon

Felt Wee Folk: Enchanting Projects, Salley Mavor

Floral Affair, A: Quilts & Accessories for Romantics, Nihon Vogue

Flowering Favorites from Piece O' Cake Designs: Becky Goldsmith & Linda Jenkins

Four Seasons in Flannel: 23 Projects—Quilts & More, Jean Wells & Lawry Thorn

Flower Pounding: Quilt Projects for All Ages, Ann Frischkorn & Amy Sandrin

Free-Style Quilts: A "No Rules" Approach, Susan Carlson

Hand Appliqué with Alex Anderson: Seven Projects for Hand Appliqué, Alex Anderson

Hand Quilting with Alex Anderson: Six Projects for First-Time Hand Quilters, Alex Anderson

Heirloom Machine Quilting, Third Edition: Comprehensive Guide to Hand-Quilting Effects Using Your Sewing Machine, Harriet Hargrave

Hidden Block Quilts: • Discover New Blocks Inside Traditional Favorites • 13 Quilt Settings • Instructions for 76 Blocks, Lerlene Nevaril

Hunter Star Quilts & Beyond: Jan Krentz

In the Nursery: Creative Quilts and Designer Touches, Jennifer Sampou & Carolyn Schmitz

Kaleidoscopes & Quilts, Paula Nadelstern

Kids Start Quilting with Alex Anderson: •7 Fun & Easy Projects •Quilts for Kids by Kids •Tips for Quilting with Children, Alex Anderson

Laurel Burch Quilts: Kindred Creatures, Laurel Burch

Liberated String Quilts, Gwen Marston

Lone Star Quilts & Beyond: Step-by-Step Projects and Inspiration, Jan Krentz

Luscious Landscapes: Simple Techniques for Dynamic Quilts, Joyce R. Becker

Machine Embroidery and More: Ten Step-by-Step Projects Using Border Fabrics & Beads, Kristen Dibbs

Magical Four-Patch and Nine-Patch Quilts, Yvonne Porcella

Make it Simpler Paper Piecing: Easy as 1-2-3 — A Pinless Fold & Sew Technique, Anita Grossman Solomon

Mariner's Compass Quilts: New Directions, Judy Mathieson

Mary Mashuta's Confetti Quilts: A No-Fuss Approach to Color, Fabric & Design, Mary Mashuta

Mastering Machine Appliqué, 2nd Edition: The Complete Guide Including: • Invisible Machine Appliqué • Satin Stitch • Blanket Stitch & Much More, Harriet Hargrave

Mastering Quilt Marking: Marking Tools and Techniques, Choosing Stencils, Matching Borders and Corners, Pepper Cory

New Look at Log Cabin Quilts, A: Design a Scene Block by Block PLUS 10 Easy-to-Follow Projects, Flavin Glover

Paper Piecing Picnic: Fun-Filled Projects for Every Quilter, From the Editors and Contributors of Quilter's Newsletter Magazine and Quiltmaker Magazine

Paper Piecing Potpourri: Fun-Filled Projects for Every Quilter, From the Editors and Contributors of Quilter's Newsletter Magazine and Quiltmaker Magazine

Patchwork Persuasion: Fascinating Quilts from Traditional Designs, Joen Wolfrom

Patchwork Quilts Made Easy—Revised, 2nd Edition: 33 Quilt Favorites, Old & New, Jean Wells

Perfect Union of Patchwork & Appliqué, A, Darlene Christopherson

Pieced Flowers, Ruth B. McDowell

Piecing: Expanding the Basics, Ruth B. McDowell

Provence Quilts and Cuisine, Marie-Christine Flocard & Cosabeth Parriaud

Q is for Quilt, Diana McClun & Laura Nownes

Quick-Strip Paper Piecing: For Blocks, Borders & Quilts, Peggy Martin

Quick Quilts for the Holidays: 11 Projects to Stamp, Stencil, and Sew, Trice Boerens

Quilting Back to Front: Fun & Easy No-Mark Techniques, Larraine Scouler

Quilting with Carol Armstrong: •30 Quilting Patterns•Appliqué Designs•16 Projects, Carol Armstrong

Quilts, Quilts, and More Quilts!, Diana McClun & Laura Nownes

Radiant New York Beauties: 14 Paper-Pieced Quilt Projects, Valori Wells

Rag Wool Appliqué: •Easy to Sew •Use Any Sewing Machine •Quilts, Home Decor & Clothing, Kathy MacMannis

Reverse Appliqué with No Brakez, Jan Mullen

Ricky Tims' Convergence Quilts: Mysterious, Magical, Easy, and Fun, Ricky Tims

Rotary Cutting with Alex Anderson: Tips, Techniques, and Projects, Alex Anderson

Say It with Quilts, Diana McClun & Laura Nownes

Scrap Quilts: The Art of Making Do, Roberta Horton

Shoreline Quilts: 15 Glorious Get-Away Projects, compiled by Cyndy Rymer

Show Me How to Machine Quilt: A Fun, No-Mark Approach, Kathy Sandbach

Simple Fabric Folding for Christmas: 14 Festive Quilts & Projects, Liz Aneloski

Slice of Christmas from Piece O' Cake Designs, A, Linda Jenkins & Becky Goldsmith

Smashing Sets: Exciting Ways to Arrange Quilt Blocks, Margaret J. Miller

Snowflakes & Quilts, Paula Nadelstern

Start Quilting with Alex Anderson, 2nd Edition: Six Projects for First-Time Quilters, Alex Anderson

Stitch 'n Flip Quilts: 14 Fantastic Projects, Valori Wells

Strips 'n Curves: A New Spin on Strip Piecing, Louisa L. Smith

Sweet Dreams, Moon Baby: A Quilt to Make, A Story to Read, Elly Sienkiewicz

Teddy Bear Redwork: •25 Fresh, New Designs •Step-by-Step Projects •Quilts and More, Jan Rapacz

Tradition with a Twist: Variations on Your Favorite Quilts, Blanche Young & Dalene Young-Stone

Trapunto by Machine, Hari Walner

Wildflowers: Designs for Appliqué and Quilting, Carol Armstrong

Wine Country Quilts: A Bounty of Flavorful Projects for Any Palette, Cyndy Lyle Rymer & Jennifer Rounds

When Quilters Gather: 20 Patterns of Piecers at Play, Ruth B. McDowell

For more information, ask for a free catalog:

C&T Publishing, Inc.
P.O. Box 1456, Lafayette, CA 94549
(800) 284-1114
Email: ctinfo@ctpub.com   Website: www.ctpub.com

For quilting supplies:

Cotton Patch Mail Order
3405 Hall Lane, Dept.CTB,
Lafayette, CA 94549
(800) 835-4418   (925) 283-7883
Email: quiltusa@yahoo.com
Website: www.quiltusa.com

Great American Quilt Factory
8970 E. Hampden Ave.
Denver, CO 80231
(800) 474-2665
Email: info@greatamericanquilt.com
Website: www.greatamericanquilt.com

Note: Fabrics used in the quilts shown may not be currently available since fabric manufacturers keep most fabrics in print for only a short time.